FATIMA
IN
LUCIA'S OWN WORDS

SISTER LUCIA'S MEMOIRS

Edited by
FR. LOUIS KONDOR, SVD.

Introduced by
DR. JOAQUIN M. ALONSO, CMF.

Translated by
Dominican Nuns of Perpetual Rosary

Distributed by
The Ravengate Press
Box 103
Cambridge, Massachusetts 02138

POSTULATION CENTRE, FATIMA, PORTUGAL

PREFACE

by the Editor

An English edition of the Memoirs of Sister Mary Lucia of the Immaculate Heart requires not only the introduction necessary for any book, but also a few comments from the editor.

For various reasons, Sister Lucia's Memoirs represent indeed one of the most outstanding works of Catholic literature in our times. First, this book bears the richest, most comprehensive and most vivid witness to the happenings in the Cova da Iria that we possess. The reader is carried away by the charm of a pure and unpretentious style of writing, which is always inspired by the most delicate religious feeling and the most sincere conviction. The whole of her style — at times filtered through a feminine soul formed by a conventual spirituality — shows that her words spring forth spontaneously, without forced literary devices.

This book, therefore, is destined to create something of a new climate within souls, which they will find at once pleasant and comforting. The invasion of secularism has caused an icy wind to blow through the Church of God today, which chills the heart. Instead of the «New Pentecost» longed for by Pope John XXIII, we are living through the hard, cold winter, so deplored by his successor, Pope Paul VI.

What souls need nowadays is to drink from the pure, clear waters which flow from the deep wellspring of a new understanding of the Gospel. Through these reminiscences of Sister Lucia, Fatima becomes for us a cooling spring, a breath of pure mountain air, that refreshes us as we journey through the desert to the Promised Land. The reading of this book, therefore, is destined to impart a deep peace to troubled minds in this day and age. The good tidings of Bethlehem echo in Fatima: «Do not be afraid; I am the Angel of Peace».

For these reasons, we have made every effort to incorporate into this edition the best elements available. By kind permission of the Most Reverend Bishop of Leiria, we had the original manuscripts at our disposal, and on these our translation has been based. We have been guided by the desire to be faithful, not only to the literal meaning of the text, but also to its spiritual content.

We have, therefore, entrusted the work of this translation to the care of the English speaking community of Dominican Nuns of the Perpetual Rosary of the Monastery Pius XII, Fatima. The nuns live out their cloistered lives on the very ground where the little shepherds used to pass with their flocks. These daughters of Saint Dominic are contemplatives who, through their offering of penance and prayer, and particularly the prayer of the Rosary, make unceasing supplication for humanity. This constitutes, in the words of Pope Pius XII, «the most beautiful response to the desires which the Mother of God deigned to express to the little seers». Breathing the very atmosphere of the Cova da Iria, they seek to communicate the Message of Fatima in various ways, among others through translations. We feel that this renders them particularly apt translators of Lucia's Memoirs.

We have asked for the collaboration of the leading authority on Fatima, the Rev. Dr. Joaquin Maria Alonso, CMF., because it was necessary to place the text in its proper setting, with due regard to the circumstances prevailing at the time. He wrote the following:

— a general introduction to the Memoirs;
— a brief biographical sketch of Sister Lucia, up to the time when she left the Institute of the Sisters of St. Dorothy, to which she had belonged until then, in order to enter the Convent of the Discalced Carmelites in Coimbra, where she still continues to live her life of silence and prayer;
— a short literary foreword: Lucia's literary qualities;
      Reminiscences — a literary form;
— an introduction to each Memoir;
— logical and systematic sub-titles which never misrepresent the tenor of the work, but make its reading more pleasant, intelligible and meaningful;
— several notes, but not too many, as required for the understanding of difficult parts of the text;
— finally, we have asked Dr. Alonso to check the translation, in order to obtain his expert judgment as to whether the text corresponds exactly to the Portuguese original wording.

Dr. Alonso has performed all these tasks with his own detailed and *deliberate experience. We should like to thank him, not only on our own behalf, but also on behalf of the many readers who will benefit from his valuable work.*

Our edition therefore guarantees, in every respect, that the words of Sister Lucia will reach, and make a deep impression upon, the very hearts of the readers.

Finally, we must thank Our Lord for the unique grace of being able to transmit to our readers a work which will help them to grow in the knowledge and love of the holy Mother of God and our Mother.

Fr. Louis Kondor, SVD.,
Postulator for the Causes of Beatification
of Francisco and Jacinta.

13th May, 1976.

FOREWORD

by Dr. Joaquin M. Alonso, CMF.

INTRODUCTION TO SISTER LUCIA'S MEMOIRS

Before a proper introduction to the entire publication of the Memoirs, the reader will appreciate a short presentation of our intentions, the limits we have established for ourselves, and the working procedure adopted by us.

This edition of the Memoirs of Sister Lucia is a true and faithful translation of the Portuguese text of the original letters, which are kept in the Episcopal archives in Leiria. We are indebted to His Excellency the Bishop, Most Reverend Dom Alberto Cosme do Amaral, for his permission for its publication. This is, of course, not a critical edition in the real sense of the word. We are translating the original texts, and reproducing the words of the authoress herself, with every possible accuracy and reliability. The final and critical edition is to be published shortly — God willing — as a detailed work, entitled, «Dr. Joaquin Alonso — Fatima: Critical Studies and Texts».

The present work is, therefore, a popular and simple edition of a valuable text, which will astonish the world. We are not calling it «popular» in order to be exempted from the demands of literary criticism, even though we do not wish to meet all of these demands here; for instance, it is not necessary to draw our readers' attention to all the references and sources supporting our statements. They can rest assured that, in this introduction and in the notes, we shall not make any assertions which we shall not substantiate in the critical work which we hope to publish before long.

Such a «popular» work, however, must have certain limits. It is not necessary to multiply references and notes. In order that the reader may understand the text without difficulty, we are giving the necessary explanations wherever we feel that the choice of words or the train of thought of the authoress require elucidation. This is also the basis of our working procedure. We did not think it advisable to edit such texts as those of Lucia — which in themselves are exceptionally transparent and unpretentious — without making the normal divisions originating from the text itself. We have, therefore, divided the Memoirs into sections, chapters and paragraphs, as suggested by the very text itself or its logical structure. In order to make it clear to the reader that the headings have been chosen by us and not by Sister Lucia, we have had them printed in capital letters and bold type respectively. We hope in this way to provide the reader with a brief pause where the descriptions are lengthy, and that the headings will at the same time prepare the mind for the contents of what is to come. The notes at the end of each Memoir are to assist the reader in overcoming certain difficulties, i.e. to explain various circumstances that appear strange at first, or other points without which some aspects of the original text cannot be understood.

In the first place, we are presenting a brief, though as yet unfinished, biography of Sister Lucia, followed by a description of her literary abilities, and finally a general introduction to her Memoirs.

A BIOGRAPHICAL SKETCH OF LUCIA

«On the 30th day of March, 1907, a female child was baptised, of the name Lucia, born at Aljustrel... on the 22nd day of March of the same year, at 7 o'clock in the evening.» This is the wording shown in the Parish Register. Her parents were Antonio dos Santos and Maria Rosa, residents of Aljustrel, a hamlet belonging to the parish of Fatima.

As the youngest of seven children, six girls and one boy, Lucia was the family favourite and was surrounded with affection from her earliest childhood. Although the family met with many troubles and misfortunes, Lucia's mother bore them all in an exemplary christian spirit. At the age of six, Lucia received her first Holy Communion, the account of which will move our readers to joy and wonder. Family circumstances obliged her to start out in life straight away as a shepherdess. At first, in 1915, her companions were the girls and boys of Aljustrel and its surroundings. As from 1917, her cousins Jacinta and Francisco Marto were her sole companions. That was the year in which the Blessed Virgin appeared. Lucia had a special role during the apparitions, as the Vision spoke only to her, and gave her a message which was only to be revealed at a future date. She lived and suffered, together with Francisco and Jacinta, on account of the apparitions. She alone has remained on earth for a longer period, in order to fulfil her mission.

The Blessed Virgin actually requested her to learn to read... She started attending school, however, only after the apparitions; but with her talents and her good memory she learned to read and write very quickly.

As soon as the apparitions were over, of course, Lucia found herself in the position of a «visionary», with all the dangers resulting therefrom. Something, therefore, had to be done about her. One of the primary interests of the new Bishop of the re-established Diocese of Leiria was her education; he tried to keep her away from the dangers threatening her in an atmosphere so permeated with the extraordinary. On the morning of June 17th, 1921, she entered the College of the Sisters of St. Dorothy at Vilar, which is now a suburb of Porto. We are giving a description of what she looked like in those days which, by the way, corresponds perfectly to the well-known photographs: «High and broad head; large brown, lively eyes; thin eye--brows; flat nose, wide mouth, thick lips, round chin. The face radiates something supernatural. Hair light and fine; of slight build, but tall for her age: 13 years and six months. Strong features, but a likeable face. Lively, intelligent, but modest and without presumption. Hands of normal size, roughened by work.»

As a young girl of 14 years and three months, Lucia entered the College of Porto, and there she received an excellent moral and religious formation. Her schooling was rather inadequate however, as it went barely beyond elementary levels. From the beginning, she was thoroughly trained in domestic work. Nevertheless, with her great ability, her good memory, her perseverance and her serious behaviour, this young girl succeeded in acquiring a fairly complete education.

Even before she entered the College, Lucia already felt drawn to dedicate herself to God in the religious life. The intensely pious life of the College, however, caused her to reflect more deeply, and her first thought went to the Carmelites... But the example of her teachers and her gratitude towards them made her decide to enter the Institute of St. Dorothy. The Portuguese Novitiate was at that time, 1921-1925, at Tuy, where Lucia entered on October 24th, 1925, at the age of 18. She went first to the house at Pontevedra, where she spent some months as a postulant. This house was situated in a side street known as «Travesia de Isabella II», and there she stayed from the 25th October, 1925, to the 20th July, 1926. She then went to the Novitiate House of Tuy to complete her postulancy, and began her novitiate with her Clothing on 2nd October, 1926. After two years, she made her profession of Vows on the 3rd October, 1928. She remained on in the same house, but with the professed Sisters, until she took her Perpetual Vows on the 3rd October, 1934. A few days later, she was transferred to the Convent of Pontevedra and only returned to Tuy in May, 1937, where she remained until she was sent to Portugal at the end of May, 1946.

After a few days' visit to the Cova da Iria and Aljustrel, where she identified the places of the Apparitions, Sister Lucia was assigned to the house at Sardão in Vila Nova de Gaia near Porto. And finally, when the desire she had had for a long time to live in seclusion and solitude re-awakened, she received, by kind favour of Pope Pius XII, permission to change over to the Discalced Carmelites, whom she joined on March 25th, 1948. And there, ever since, she has been living a life of prayer and penance. Pilgrims on their way to Fatima, who pass through Coimbra to visit the Carmel there, may hear her voice in the nuns' choir of the Discalced Carmelites. Now, in 1976, Sister Mary Lucia of the Immaculate Heart is 69 years of age.

LUCIA'S LITERARY QUALITIES

With regard to everything written concerning Fatima, one cannot but agree with what the Portuguese writer, Antero de Figueiredo, enthusiastically wrote about his own book: «But the light, the wonderful light of this book, has its origin in the pure, deep and admirably simple soul of the seer, Lucia of Jesus.» First of all, let us mention that Lucia's manuscripts do indeed reveal a certain lack of literary education. However, Lucia's great natural talents have made up for what would otherwise have been a deficiency that could scarcely have been remedied. She admits more than once and quite openly how «incapable and inadequate» she is. To quote her own words, she says: «Even my handwriting is scarcely presentable». Whatever her deficiency, it does not impede her clear and distinct construction of sentences; sometimes indeed, she writes in an elegant and elevated style.

Her literary qualities could be summarized as follows: accuracy and clarity of thought; delicate and deep feeling; lively imagination and a truly artistic sense of humour, giving charm to the narrative; a sensitive irony that never hurts; an extraordinary memory as far as details and circumstances are concerned. Lucia's dialogues pour forth as though the people concerned were present in person. In her imagination, she sees the scenery as if it were before her eyes. She describes Jacinta and Francisco, her confessors and others, with words which disclose an unusual psychological insight. She is fully conscious of her deviations, and always returns with much skill to her starting-point.

In a way, her style is influenced occasionally by the somewhat flowery conventual literature, but her naturalness, vivacity and joy always triumph. Who could forget that last night when she bade

11

farewell to the beloved places where the apparitions occurred, on the eve of her departure for Porto? Who could not admire the graceful way in which she describes the shoes of a certain Canon with their silver buckles? How could anybody not be surprised at the ease with which she records those «Songs of the Mountains»?

From the very beginning, Lucia knows how to express what she wants to say, and she says it in her own way. Aided by her vivid imagination, she succeeds in writing what she wants to write, and even if domestic work momentarily distracts her, she continues her writing without interrupting either a coherent narrative or the logic of her reflections. Something like that would not be possible without great mental composure.

It is true that Lucia felt «inspired» to write, as she frequently mentions... Her conviction that she could feel a Divine Presence when writing must not be understood in the strict sense of the word «inspiration», i.e. in the nature of prophecy, as a hairsplitting critic described it. She feels that in writing she is «helped» by God. A careful reading of her work, however, makes one recognise immediately that Lucia does not mean to use such words in their fullest sense. She herself gives us an explicit answer by saying: «The word 'inspired' indicates that there is a mental stimulus to our actions».

Therefore, it is not a question of «inerrancy» as applied to Holy Scripture. Lucia may be deceived in the mystical interpretation of her experiences, because of the very difficulty of such «interpretation». At times, she herself is in doubt as to whether it is God who is talking to her; at other times, she confesses that it would be impossible to make known something which she has experienced through a mystical grace. Intelligent criticism will discover some mistakes in dates, events and circumstances. Even if she assures us in critical moments that she is indeed giving us «ipsissima verba», i.e. the very words of the Blessed Virgin herself, this really means nothing other than her effort to be as honest as possible. What Lucia always feels sure about — and she says so — is the meaning of her words.

As far as dates are concerned, Lucia's uncertainty is well known; for one thing, she, Francisco and Jacinta, being children, could count neither days nor months, not to mention years. Thus Lucia has no recollection of the dates on which the angel appeared; she can only remember them approximately on account of the seasons, which made a strong impression on these small mountain children. The main reason for this weaker aspect of her memory can certainly be found in the realistic character of Lucia's reminiscences, which is always directed towards the essential.

Moreover, the reader of Lucia's reminiscences must not forget a guiding principle governing the interpretation of the messages, which mystics receive in connection with their supernatural experiences: it is always a question of «interpretation», and this does not necessarily mean that everything which the mystics say, corresponds word for word to the Divine Messages. This does not imply, however, that one should only believe in what is merely natural in the extraordinary phenomena she experienced.

We should like to point out a final difficulty, so that the reader will be better prepared for reading these wonderful texts. One has to differentiate between a Message from Heaven as presented to us by Sister Lucia, and the «reflection» on it or «interpretation» of it given by her.

Within the difficulties inherent in mystical interpretation, the former gives us a greater guarantee of truthfulness than the latter. If God has given such obvious signs, in order to manifest His Presence in the events at Fatima, then it can be taken for granted that He also intervened in a special manner, so that His Message, transmitted through Mary, would be faithfully passed on by the little seers chosen for that purpose. As we assert that God has given a Message of Salvation to His Church, we must also accept that He has bestowed upon it the charism of Truth to pass this Message on to us without error. We often observe Lucia «thinking» about words and events... She is thereby a privileged interpreter, but only and always an interpreter. In this regard, therefore, Sister Lucia's words need not have that special assistance which we claim for the first-mentioned case.

THE KIND OF LITERATURE CALLED «REMINISCENCES»

We are calling the manuscripts which we place before the reader «reminiscences», because they are indeed most similar to this kind of literature, even if they sometimes look like letters or autobiographies. From the outset, Sister Lucia had no literary ambition in the writing of these admirable documents. She wrote because she was requested to do so. We can rest assured that she has never written anything of her own accord. That does not mean that, in the course of her work, she is not carried away occasionally by the events she mentions, or by the impression that she is indeed creating «literature». However, this literature is always clear and spontaneous, and an elegant style emerges without effort or intention on her part.

Sister Lucia was in nowise concerned about the kind of literature she was writing, and she had no idea at all that the word «reminiscences» could mean anything other than memory. She mentions once that she did not know how to carry out the order she had received to give an account of Jacinta's life, and therefore quite naturally turned to the Bishop as if she were telling him a story based on her own recollections.. Therefore, these manuscripts addressed to the Bishop of Leiria should not be regarded as long letters. This procedure was a mere fiction, a literary one in this case, in order to get out of the difficulty. What Lucia really wants is to write down her reminiscences, and for that reason they are entitled to be called «reminiscences», because this is indeed a kind of literature in which the author wants to convey recollections relating to himself or others, to his own expeperience or to that of others.

By no means, however, could these manuscripts be called a biography or autobiography in the strict sense of the word. Lucia did not and could not intend to submit to us either a biography of Jacinta or Francisco, or an autobiography. It was only a question of a number of recollections relating to the principal facts in the lives of Jacinta and of Francisco and, of course, of Lucia herself as well, although it was not her intention to dwell on herself.

Biography and autobiography, however, differ from «reminiscences», inasmuch as the latter does not wish to convey more than just reminiscences. The former kinds of literature aim at something more complete and systematic, and are based, not on mere recollections, but on an analysis of documents. In her work, however, Lucia had only to look back and write down her recollectionsl Since these concerned the lives of Francisco and Jacinta, they inevitably concerned her own as well. On the other hand, everything connected with the apparitions of the Lady was seen no longer as a simple recollection, but as a presence impressed upon her soul as though by fire. She herself points out to us that these things remain impressed upon her soul in such a way that she could not possibly forget them.

These reminiscences of Sister Lucia, therefore, are rather like re-reading inscriptions which are forever engraven in the deepest depths of the soul of the authoress. She appears to be «seeing» rather than «remembering». The ease of her «remembering» is indeed so great that she has only to «read», as it were, from her soul.

FIRST MEMOIR

Introduction

This is certainly not the first manuscript we have from Sister Lucia's pen, but it is the first long document that she wrote. Previously, we have had letters, many letters in fact, interrogations, reports and so on; but now we have a long and important document before us. If Lucia has not written it of her own accord, how then has it been accomplished?

On 12th September, 1935, the mortal remains of Jacinta were taken from Vila Nova de Ourém to the cemetery of Fatima. On this occasion various photographs were taken of the body, one of which was sent by the Bishop to Sister Lucia, who was at that time in the convent of Pontevedra. On 17th November, 1935, Lucia, writing in acknowledgement, said among other things: «Thank you very much for the photographs. I can never express how much I value them, especially those of Jacinta. I felt like removing the wrappings in order to see all of her... I was so enraptured! My joy at seeing the closest friend of my childhood again was so great... She was a child only in years. As to the rest, she already knew how to be virtuous, and to show God and the most holy Virgin her love through sacrifice...»

These very vivid recollections of her small cousin, Jacinta, caused the Bishop to request Lucia to write down everything she could still remember about her. The manuscript, which she began during the second week of December, was actually completed on Christmas Day, 1935, that is, in less than a fortnight. This manuscript which Lucia composed forms a perfect whole; it presents a picture of Jacinta, whose soul is illumined through and through by the very light of Fatima, the Immaculate Heart of Mary.

The main purpose of this manuscript is to give us a picture of

Jacinta as it is reflected in Lucia's reminiscences. Consequently, she did not intend to write a «story» of the Apparitions for us. These form, as it were, a frame from which the picture of Jacinta shines forth. The language throughout is simple, and even, one might say, childlike at times, whenever the context calls for it. Lucia never lost her flair for realism, whatever the events she was describing.

J. M. J.
Your Excellency, '

PROLOGUE

Prayer and Obedience

Having implored the protection of the most holy Hearts of Jesus and of Mary, our tender Mother, and sought light and grace at the foot of the Tabernacle, so as to write nothing that would not be solely and exclusively for the glory of Jesus and of the most Blessed Virgin, I now take up this work, in spite of the repugnance I feel, since I can say almost nothing about Jacinta without speaking either directly or indirectly about my miserable self. I obey, nevertheless, the will of Your Excellency, which, for me, is the expression of the will of our good God. I begin this task, then, asking the most holy Hearts of Jesus and Mary to deign to bless it, and to make use of this act of obedience to obtain the conversion of poor sinners, for whom Jacinta so generously sacrificed herself.

I know Your Excellency does not expect a well-written account from me, for you know how incapable and inadequate I am. I am going to tell you, then, what I can remember about this soul, for by God's grace I was her most intimate confidante. I have such a high regard for her holiness, that I greatly esteem and respect her and dearly cherish her memory.

Keeping Secrets

In spite of my good will to be obedient, I trust Your Excellency will permit me to withhold certain matters concerning myself as well as Jacinta, that I would not wish to be read before I enter eternity. You will not find it strange that I should reserve for eternity certain secrets and other

Exmo e R.^{mo} Senhor Bispo

Depois de ter implorado a protecção dos Santíssimos Corações de Jesus e Maria, numa terna Mãe, de ter pedido luz e graça aos pés do Sacrário, para não escrever nada que não seja única e exclusivamente para a glória de Jesus e da Santíssima Virgem; venho, apesar da minha repugnancia, por não poder dizer quase nada da Jacinta sem directa ou indirectamente falar do meu miseravel ser. Obedeço instanto à vontade de V. Ex.^{cia} R.^{ma} que para mim é a expressão da vontade de Deus. Com Deus começo pois este trabalho, pedindo aos Santíssimos Corações de Jesus e Maria que se dignem abençoá-lo e servir-se d'este acto de obdiência para a conversão dos pobres pecadores, pelos quais esta alma tanto se sacrificou.

Sei que V. Ex.^{cia} R.^{ma} não espera de mim um escrito capaz pois conhece a minha incapacidade e insuficiencia, irei pois contando a V.^a Ex.^{cia} R.^{ma} o que me for recordando d'esta alma, da qual o nosso bom Deus, que fez a graça de ser a mais intima confidente; e da qual conservo a maior saudade estima e respeito, pela alta ideia que tenho da sua santidade.

Apesar Exmo e R.^{mo} Senhor Bispo da minha bôa vontade em obedecer, peço que concedais reservar, algumas coisas, que porque também me dizem respeito desejaria fossem lidas somente nos lumiares da eternidade. V. Ex.^{cia} R.^{ma} não estranhará, que pretenda guardar segredos

matters. After all, is it not the Blessed Virgin herself who sets me the example? Does not the Holy Gospel tell us that Mary kept all things in her heart? [2] And who better than this Immaculate Heart could have revealed to us the secrets of Divine Mercy? Nonetheless, she kept them to herself as in a garden enclosed, and took them with her to the palace of the Divine King.

I remember, besides, a saying that I heard from a holy priest, when I was only eleven years old. Like so many others, he came to question me, and asked among other things, about a matter of which I did not wish to speak. After he had exhausted his whole repertoire of questions, without succeeding in obtaining a satisfactory answer on this subject, realizing perhaps that he was touching on too delicate a matter, the good priest gave me his blessing and said: «You are right, my child. The secret of the king's daughter should remain hidden in the depths of her heart.»

At the time, I did not understand the meaning of what he said, but I realized that he approved of my manner of acting. I did not forget his words, however, and I understand them now. This saintly priest was at that time Vicar of Torres Novas [3]. Little does he know all the good that these few words did for my soul, and that is why I remember him with such gratitude.

One day, however, I sought the advice of a holy priest regarding my reserve in such matters, because I did not know how to answer when they asked me if the most Blessed Virgin had not told me anything else as well. This priest, who was then Vicar of Olival [4], said to us: «You do well, my little ones, to keep the secret of your souls between God and yourselves. When they put that question to you, just answer: 'Yes, she did say more, but it's a secret'. If they question you further on this subject, think of the secret that this Lady made known to you, and say: 'Our Lady told us not to say anything to anybody; for this reason, we are saying nothing.' In this way, you can keep your secret under cover of Our Lady's.»

How well I understood the explanation and guidance of this venerable old priest!

I am already taking too much time with these preliminaries, and Your Excellency will be wondering what is the purpose of it all. I must see if I can make a start with my account of what I can remember of Jacinta's life. As I have no free time at my disposal, I must make the most of the hours when we work in silence, to recall and jot down, with the aid of paper and pencil which I keep hidden under my sewing, all that the most holy Hearts of Jesus and Mary want me to remember.

To Jacinta

> Swift through the world
> You went a-flying,
> Dearest Jacinta,
> In deepest suffering
> Jesus loving.
> Forget not my plea
> And prayer to you:
> Be ever my friend
> Before the throne
> Of the Virgin Mary,
> Lily of candour,
> Shining pearl,
> Up there in heaven
> You live in glory,
> Seraphim of love,
> With your little brother
> At the Master's feet
> Pray for me. [5]

1. JACINTA'S CHARACTER

Her Natural Characteristics

Your Excellency,

Before the happenings of 1917, apart from the ties of relationship that united us, no other particular affection led me to prefer the companionship of Jacinta and Francisco to that of any other child. On the contrary, I sometimes found Jacinta's company quite disagreeable, on account of her over-sensitive temperament. The slightest quarrel which arose among the children when at play was enough to send her pouting into a corner — «tethering the donkey» as we used to say. Even the coaxing and caressing that children know so well how to give on such occasions, were still not enough to bring her back to play; she herself had to be allowed to choose the game, and her partner as well. Her heart, however, was well disposed. God had endowed her with a sweet and gentle character which made her at once lovable and attractive. I don't know why, but Jacinta and her brother Francisco had a special liking for me, and almost always came in search of me when they wanted to play. They did not enjoy the company of the other children, and they used to ask me to go with them to the well down at the bottom of the garden belonging to my parents.

Once we arrived there, Jacinta chose which games we were to play. The ones she liked best were usually «pebbles» and «buttons», which we played as we sat on the stone slabs covering the well, in the shade of an olive tree and two plum trees. Playing «buttons» often left me in great distress, because when they called us in to meals, I used to find myself minus my buttons. More often than not, Jacinta had won them all, and this was enough to make my mother scold me. I had to sew them on again in a hurry. But how could I persuade Jacinta to give them back to me, since besides her pouty ways she had another little defect: she was possessive! She wanted to keep all the buttons for the next game, so as to avoid taking off her own! It was only by threatening never to play with her again that I succeeded in getting them back!

Not a few times, I found myself unable to do what my little friend wanted. One of my older sisters was a weaver and the other a seamstress, and both were at home all day. The neighbours, therefore, used to ask my mother if they could leave their children in my parents' yard, while they themselves went out to work in the fields. The children stayed with me and played, while my sisters kept an eye on us. My mother was always willing to do this, although it meant considerable waste of time for my sisters. I was therefore charged with amusing the children, and watching to see that they did not fall into the pool in the yard. Three large figtrees sheltered the children from the scorching sun. We used their branches for swings, and an old threshing floor for a dining room. On days like these, when Jacinta came with her brother to invite me to go with them to our favourite nook, I used to tell them I could not go, because my mother had ordered me to stay where I was. Then, disappointed but resigned, the two little ones joined in our games. At siesta time, my mother used to give her children their catechism lessons, especially when Lent was drawing near, for as she said:

«I don't want to be ashamed of you, when the priest questions you on your catechism at Easter time.»

All the other children, therefore, were present at our catechism lessons and Jacinta was there as well.

Her sensitiveness

One day, one of these children accused another of improper talk. My mother reproved him very severely, pointing out that one does not say such nasty things, because they are sinful and displease the Child Jesus; and that those who commit such sins and don't confess them, go to hell. Little Jacinta did not forget the lesson. The very next time the children came, she said:

«Will your mother let you go today?»

«No.»

«Then I'm going with Francisco over to our yard.»

«And why won't you stay here?»

«My mother doesn't want us to stay when those other children are here. She told us to go and play in our own yard. She doesn't want me to learn these nasty things, which are sins and which the Child Jesus doesn't like.»

Then she whispered in my ear:

«If your mother lets you, will you come to my house?»

«Yes.»

«Then go and ask her.»

And taking her brother by the hand, she went home.

Speaking of Jacinta's favourite games, one of them was «forfeits». As Your Excellency probably knows, the loser has to do whatever the winner tells him. Jacinta loved to send the loser chasing after butterflies, to catch one and bring it to her. At other times, she demanded some flower of her own choosing. One day, we were playing forfeits at my home, and I won, so this time it was I who told her what to do. My brother was sitting at a table, writing. I told her to give him a hug and a kiss, but she protested:

«That, no! Tell me to do some other thing. Why don't you tell me to go and kiss Our Lord over there?»

There was a crucifix hanging on the wall.

«Alright», I answered, «get up on a chair, bring the crucifix over here, kneel down and give Him three hugs and three kisses: one for Francisco, one for me, and the other for yourself.»

«To Our Lord, yes, I'll give as many as you like», and she ran to get the crucifix. She kissed it and hugged it with such devotion that I have never forgotten it. Then, looking attentively at the figure of Our Lord, she asked:

«Why is Our Lord nailed to a cross like that?»

«Because He died for us.»

Tell me how it happened», she said.

Her Love for the Crucified Saviour

In the evenings my mother used to tell stories. My father and my older sisters told us fairy stories about magic spells, princesses robed in gold and royal doves. Then along came my mother with stories of the Passion, St. John the Baptist, and so on. That is how I came to know the story of Our Lord's Passion. As it was enough for me to have heard a story once, to be able to repeat it in all its details, I began to tell my companions, word for word, what I used to call Our Lord's Story. Just then, my sister [6] passed by, and noticed that we had the crucifix [7] in our hands. She took it from us and scolded us, saying that she did not want us to touch such holy things. Jacinta got up and approached my sister, saying:

«Maria, don't scold her! I did it. But I won't do it again».

My sister caressed her, and told us to go and play outside, because we left nothing in the house in its proper place. Off we went to continue our story down at the well I have already mentioned. As it was hidden behind some chestnut trees and a heap of stones and brambles, we chose this spot some years later for our more intimate talks, our fervent prayers, and to tell you everything, our tears as well — and sometimes very bitter tears they were. We mingled our tears with the waters of the same well from which we drank. Does not this make the well itself an image of Mary, in whose Heart we dried our tears and drank of the purest consolation?

But, let us come back to our story. When the little one heard me telling of the sufferings of Our Lord, she was moved to tears. From then on, she often asked me to tell it to her all over again. She would weep and grieve, saying:

«Our poor dear Lord! I'll never sin again! I don't want Our Lord to suffer any more!»

23

Her Delicate Sensibility

Jacinta also loved going out at nightfall to the threshing floor situated close to the house; there she watched the beautiful sunsets, and contemplated the starry skies. She was enraptured with the lovely moonlit nights. We vied with each other to see who could count the most stars. We called the stars Angels' lamps, the moon Our Lady's lamp and the sun Our Lord's. This led Jacinta to remark sometimes:

«You know, I like Our Lady's lamp better; it doesn't burn us up or blind us, the way Our Lord's does.»

In fact, the sun can be very strong there on summer days, and Jacinta, a delicate child, suffered greatly from the heat.

She looks and learns

As my sister [8] belonged to the Sodality of the Sacred Heart of Jesus, every time a childrens' solemn Communion came round, she took me along to renew my own. On one occasion my aunt took her little daughter to see the ceremony, and Jacinta was fascinated by the «angels» strewing flowers. From that day on, she sometimes left us when we were playing, and went off to gather an apron-full of flowers. Then she came back and strewed them over me, one by one.

«Jacinta, why on earth are you doing that?»

«I'm doing what the little angels do: I'm strewing you with flowers.»

Every year, on a big feast, probably Corpus Christi, my sister used to prepare the dresses for the children chosen to represent the angels in the procession. They walked beside the canopy, strewing flowers. I was always among the ones chosen, and one day after my sister had tried on my dress, I told Jacinta all about the coming feast, and how I was going to strew flowers before Jesus. The little one begged me to ask my sister to let her go as well. The two of us went along to make our request. My sister said she could go, and tried a dress on Jacinta. At the rehearsals, she explained how we were to strew the flowers before the Child Jesus.

«Will we see Him?» asked Jacinta.

«Yes,» replied my sister, «the parish priest will be carrying Him.»

Jacinta jumped for joy, and kept on asking how much

longer we had to wait for the feast. The longed-for day arrived at last, and Jacinta was beside herself with excitement. The two of us took our places near the altar. Later, in the procession, we walked beside the canopy, each of us with a basket of flowers. Wherever my sister had told us to strew the flowers, I strewed mine before Jesus, but in spite of all the signs I made to Jacinta, I couldn't get her to strew a single one. She kept her eyes fixed on the priest, and that was all. When the ceremony was over, my sister took us outside the church and asked:

«Jacinta, why didn't you strew your flowers before Jesus?»

«Because I didn't see Him.»

Jacinta then asked me:

«But did you see the Child Jesus?»

«Of course not. Don't you know that the Child Jesus in the Host can't be seen? He's hidden! He's the one we receive in Communion!»

«And you, when you go to Communion, do you talk to Him?»

«Yes, I do.»

«Then, why don't you see Him?»

«Because He's hidden.»

«I'm going to ask my mother to let me go to Communion too.»

«The parish priest won't let you go until you're ten years old.» [9]

«But you're not ten yet, and you go to Communion!»

«Because I knew the whole catechism, and you don't.»

After this, my two companions asked me to teach them the catechism. So I became their catechist, and they learned with exceptional enthusiasm. But though I could always answer any questions put to me, when it came to teaching, I could only remember a few things here and there. This led Jacinta to say to me one day:

«Teach us some more things; we know all those.»

I had to admit that I could remember things only when people questioned me on them, and I added:

«Ask your mother to let you go to the church to learn your catechism.»

The two children, who so ardently desired to receive the «Hidden Jesus», as they called Him, went to ask their mother, and my aunt agreed. But she rarely let them go there, for she said:

«The church is a good way from here, and you are very small. In any case, the priest won't give you Holy Communion before you're ten years old.»

Jacinta never stopped asking me questions about the Hidden Jesus, and I remember how, one day, she asked me:

«How is it that so many people receive the little Hidden Jesus at the same time? Is there one small piece for each person?»

«Not at all! Don't you see that there are many Hosts, and that there is a Child Jesus in every one of them!»

What a lot of nonsense I must have told her!

Jacinta, the Little Shepherdess

I was old enough now to be sent out to mind our sheep, just as my mother had sent her other children at my age. My sister Carolina was then thirteen, and it was time for her to go out to work. My mother, therefore, put me in charge of our flock. I passed on the news to my two companions, and told them that I would not be playing with them any more; but they could not bring themselves to accept such a separation. They went at once to ask their mother to let them come with me, but she refused. We had no alternative but to accept the separation. Nearly every day after that, they came to meet me on my way home at dusk. Then we made for the threshing floor, and ran about for a while, waiting for Our Lady and the Angels to light their lamps — or put them, as we used to say, at the window to give us light. On moonless nights, we used to say that there was no oil for Our Lady's lamp!

Jacinta and Francisco found it very hard to get used to the absence of their former companion. For this reason, they pleaded with their mother over and over again to let them, also, look after their sheep. Finally my aunt, hoping perhaps to be rid of such persistent requests, even though she knew the children were too small, handed over to them the care of their own flock. Radiant with joy, they ran to give me the news and talk over how we could put our flocks together every day. Each one was to open the pen, whenever their mother decided, and whoever reached the Barreiro first was to await the arrival of the other flock. Barreiro was the name of a pond at the bottom of the hill. As soon as we met at the pond, we decided where we would pasture the flock that day. Then off we'd go, as happy and content as if we were going to a festival.

And now, Your Excellency, we see Jacinta in her new life as a shepherdess. We won over the sheep by sharing our lunch with them. This meant that when we reached the pasture, we could play at our ease, quite sure that they would not stray far away from us. Jacinta loved to hear her voice echoing down in the valleys. For this reason, one of our favourite amusements was to climb to the top of the hills, sit down on the biggest rock we could find, and call out different names at the top of our voices. The name that echoed back most clearly was «Maria». Sometimes Jacinta used to say the whole Hail Mary this way, only calling out the following word when the preceding one had stopped re-echoing.

We loved to sing, too. Interspersed among the popular songs — of which, alas! we knew quite a number — were Jacinta's favourite hymns: «Salve Nobre Padroeira» (Hail Noble Patroness), «Virgem Pura» (Virgin Pure), «Anjos, Cantai Comigo» (Angels, sing with me). We were very fond of dancing, and any instrument we heard being played by the other shepherds was enough to set us off. Jacinta, tiny as she was, had a special aptitude for dancing.

We had been told to say the Rosary after our lunch, but as the whole day seemed too short for our play, we worked out a fine way of getting through it quickly. We simply passed the beads through our fingers, saying nothing but «Hail Mary, Hail Mary, Hail Mary...» At the end of each mystery, we paused awhile, then simply said «Our Father», and so, in the twinkling of an eye, as they say, we had our Rosary finished!

Jacinta also loved to hold the little white lambs tightly in her arms, sitting with them on her lap, fondling them, kissing them, and carrying them home at night on her shoulders, so that they wouldn't get tired. One day on her way back, she walked along in the middle of the flock.

«Jacinta, what are you doing there,» I asked her, «in the middle of the sheep?»

«I want to do the same as Our Lord in that holy picture they gave me. He's just like this, right in the middle of them all, and He's holding one of them in His arms.»

The First Apparition

And now, Your Excellency, you know more or less how Jacinta spent the first seven years of her life, right up to that 13th day of May, 1917, which dawned bright and fair like so many others before it. That day, by chance — if in the designs of Providence there can be such a thing as chance — we chose to pasture our flock on some land belonging to my parents, called Cova da Iria. We chose the pasture as we usually did, at the Barreiro I have already mentioned. This meant we had to cross a barren stretch of moorland to get there, which made the journey doubly long. We had to go slowly to give the sheep a chance to graze along the way, so it was almost noon when we arrived. I will not delay here to tell you what happened that day, because Your Excellency knows it well already, and therefore it would be a waste of time. Except for the sake of obedience, my writing this seems a waste of time to me as well. For I cannot see what good Your Excellency can draw from it all, unless it could be that you will become better acquainted with Jacinta's innocence of life.

Before beginning to tell Your Excellency what I remember of this new period of Jacinta's life, I must first admit that there were certain aspects of Our Lady's apparitions which we had agreed not to make known to anybody. Now however, I may have to speak about them in order to explain whence Jacinta imbibed such great love for Jesus, for suffering and for sinners, for whose salvation she sacrificed herself so generously. Your Excellency is not unaware that she was the one who, unable to contain herself for joy, broke our agreement to keep the whole matter to ourselves. That very afternoon, while we remained thoughtful and rapt in wonder, Jacinta kept breaking into enthusiastic exclamations:

«Oh, what a beautiful Lady!»

«I can see what's going to happen», I said, «you'll end up saying that to somebody else.»

«No, I won't», she answered, «don't worry.»

Next day, Francisco came running to tell me how she had told them everything at home the night before. Jacinta listened to the accusation without a word.

«You see, that's just what I thought would happen.» I said to her.

«There was something within me that wouldn't let me keep quiet,» she said, with tears in her eyes.

«Well, don't cry now, and don't tell anything else to anybody about what the Lady said to us.»

«But I've already told them.»

«And what did you say?»

«I said that the Lady promised to take us to heaven.»

«To think you told them that!»

«Forgive me. I won't tell anybody anything ever again!»

Reflecting on Hell

That day, when we reached the pasture, Jacinta sat thoughtfully on a rock.

«Jacinta, come and play.»

«I don't want to play today.»

«Why not?»

«Because I'm thinking. That Lady told us to say the Rosary and to make sacrifices for the conversion of sinners. So from now on, when we say the Rosary we must say the whole Hail Mary and the whole Our Father! And the sacrifices, how are we going to make them?»

Right away, Francisco thought of a good sacrifice:

«Let's give our lunch to the sheep, and make the sacrifice of doing without it.»

In a couple of minutes, the contents of our lunchbag had been divided among the sheep. So that day, we fasted as strictly as the most austere Carthusian! Jacinta remained sitting on her rock, looking very thoughtful, and asked:

«That Lady also said that many souls go to hell! What is hell, then?»

«It's like a big deep pit of wild beasts, with an enormous fire in it — that's how my mother used to explain it to me — and that's where people go who commit sins and don't confess them. They stay there and burn for ever!»

«And they never get out of there again?»

«No!»

«Not even after many, many years?»

«No! Hell never ends!»

«And heaven never ends either?»

«Whoever goes to heaven, never leaves it again!»

«And whoever goes to hell, never leaves it either?»

«They're eternal, don't you see! They never end.»

That was how, for the first time, we made a meditation on hell and eternity. What made the biggest impression on Jacinta was the idea of eternity. Even in the middle of a game, she would stop and ask:

«But listen! Doesn't hell end after many, many years, then?»

Or again:

«Those people burning in hell, don't they ever die? And don't they turn into ashes? And if people pray very much for sinners, won't Our Lord get them out of there? And if they make sacrifices as well? Poor sinners! We have to pray and make many sacrifices for them!»

Then she went on:

«How good that Lady is! She has already promised to take us to heaven!»

Conversion of Sinners

Jacinta took this matter of making sacrifices for the conversion of sinners so much to heart, that she never let a single opportunity escape her. There were two families in Moita [10], whose children used to go round begging from door to door. We met them one day, as we were going along with our sheep. As soon as she saw them, Jacinta said to us:

«Let's give our lunch to those poor children, for the conversion of sinners.»

And she ran to take it to them. That afternoon, she told me she was hungry. There were holm-oaks and oak trees nearby. The acorns were still quite green. However, I told her we could eat them. Francisco climbed up a holm-oak to fill his pockets, but Jacinta remembered that we could eat the ones on the oak trees instead, and thus make a sacrifice by eating the bitter kind. So it was there, that afternoon, that we enjoyed this delicious repast! Jacinta made this one of her usual sacrifices, and often picked the acorns off the oaks or the olives off the trees.

One day I said to her:

«Jacinta, dont eat that; it's too bitter!»

«But it's because it's bitter that I'm eating it, for the conversion of sinners.»

These were not the only times we fasted. We had agreed that whenever we met any poor children like these, we would give them our lunch. They were only too happy to receive such an alms, and they took good care to meet us; they used to wait for us along the road. We no sooner saw them than Jacinta ran to give them all the food we had for that day, as happy as if she had no need of it herself. On days like that, our only nourishment consisted of pine nuts, and little berries about the size of an olive which grow on the roots of yellow bell-flowers, as well as blackberries, mushrooms, and some other things we found on the roots of pine trees — I can't remember now what these were called. If there was fruit available on the land belonging to our parents, we used to eat that.

Jacinta's thirst for making sacrifices seemed insatiable. One day a neighbour offered my mother a good pasture for our sheep. Though it was quite far away and we were at the height of summer, my mother accepted the offer made so generously, and sent me there. She told me that we should take our siesta in the shade of the trees, as there was a pond nearby where the flock could go and drink. On the way, we met our dear poor children, and Jacinta ran to give them our usual alms. It was a lovely day, but the sun was blazing, and in that arid, stony wasteland, it seemed as though it would burn everything up. We were parched with thirst, and there wasn't a single drop of water for us to drink! At first, we offered the sacrifice generously for the conversion of sinners, but after midday, we could hold out no longer.

As there was a house quite near, I suggested to my companions that I should go and ask for a little water. They agreed to this, so I went and knocked on the door. A little old woman gave me not only a pitcher of water, but also some bread, which I accepted gratefully. I ran to share it with my little companions, and then offered the pitcher to Francisco, and told him to take a drink.

«I don't want to,» he replied.

«Why?»

«I want to suffer for the conversion of sinners.»

«You have a drink, Jacinta!»

«But I want to offer this sacrifice for sinners too.»

Then I poured the water into a hollow in the rock, so that the sheep could drink it, and went to return the pitcher to its owner. The heat was getting more and more intense. The shrill singing of the crickets and grasshoppers coupled with the croaking of the frogs in the neighbouring pond made an uproar that was almost unbearable. Jacinta, frail as she was, and weakened still more by the lack of food and drink, said to me with that simplicity which was natural to her:

«Tell the crickets and the frogs to keep quiet! I have such a terrible headache.»

Then Francisco asked her:

«Don't you want to suffer this for sinners?»

The poor child, clasping her head between her two little hands, replied:

«Yes, I do. Let them sing!»

Family Opposition

In the meantime, news of what had happened was spreading. My mother was getting worried, and wanted at all costs to make me deny what I had said. One day, before I set out with the flock, she was determined to make me confess that I was telling lies, and to this end she spared neither caresses, nor threats, nor even the broomstick. To all this she received nothing but a mute silence, or the confirmation of all that I had already said. She told me to go and let out the sheep, and during the day to consider well that she had never tolerated a single lie among her children, and much less would she allow a lie of this kind. She warned me that she would force me, that very evening, to go to those people whom I had deceived, confess that I had lied and ask their pardon.

I went off with my sheep, and that day my little companions were already waiting for me. When they saw me crying, they ran up and asked me what was the matter. I told them all that had happened, and added:

«Tell me now, what am I to do? My mother is determined at all costs to make me say that I was lying. But how can I?»

Then Francisco said to Jacinta:

«You see! It's all your fault. Why did you have to tell them?»

The poor child, in tears, knelt down, joined her hands, and asked our forgiveness:

«I did wrong» she said through her tears, «but I will never tell anything to anybody again.»

Your Excellency will probably be wondering who taught Jacinta to make such an act of humility? I don't know. Perhaps she had seen her brothers and sisters asking their parents' forgiveness before going to Communion; or else, as I think myself, Jacinta was the one who received from Our Lady a greater abundance of grace, and a better knowledge of God and of virtue.

When the parish priest [II] sent for us some time later, to question us, Jacinta put her head down, and only with difficulty did he succeed in getting a word or two out of her. Once outside, I asked her:

«Why didn't you answer the priest?»

«Because I promised you never to tell anything to anybody again!»

One day she asked:

«Why can't we say that the Lady told us to make sacrifices for sinners?»

«So they won't be asking what kind of sacrifices we are making.»

My mother became more and more upset at the way things were progressing. This led her to make yet another attempt to force me to confess that I had lied. One morning early, she called me and told me she was taking me to see the parish priest, saying:

«When you get there, go down on your knees, tell him that you've lied, and ask his pardon.»

As we were going past my aunt's house, my mother went inside for a few minutes. This gave me a chance to tell Jacinta what was happening. Seeing me so upset, she shed some tears and said:

«I'm going to get up and call Francisco. We'll go and pray for you at the well. When you get back, come and find us there.»

On my return, I ran to the well, and there were the two of them on their knees, praying. As soon as they saw me, Jacinta ran to hug me, and then she said:

«You see! We must never be afraid of anything! The Lady will help us always. She's such a good friend of ours!»

Ever since the day Our Lady taught us to offer our sacrifices to Jesus, any time we had something to suffer, or agreed to make a sacrifice, Jacinta asked:

«Did you already tell Jesus that it's for love of Him?»

If I said I hadn't, she answered:

«Then I'll tell Him,» and joining her hands, she raised her eyes to heaven and said:

«Oh Jesus, it is for love of You, and for the conversion of sinners!»

Love for the Holy Father

Two priests, who had come to question us, recommended that we pray for the Holy Father. Jacinta asked who the Holy Father was. The good priests explained who he was and how much he needed prayers. This gave Jacinta such love for the Holy Father that, every time she offered her sacrifices to Jesus, she added: «and for the Holy Father». At the end of the Rosary, she always said three Hail Marys for the Holy Father, and sometimes she would remark:

«How I'd love to see the Holy Father! So many people come here, but the Holy Father never does!» [12]

In her childish simplicity, she supposed that the Holy Father could make this journey just like anybody else!

One day, my father and my uncle [13] were summoned to appear next morning with the three of us before the Administrator. [14]

«I'm not going to take my children,» announced my uncle, «nor present them before any tribunal. Why, they're not old enough to be responsible for their actions, and besides all that, they could never stand the long journey on foot to Vila Nova de Ourém. I'll go myself and see what they want.»

My father thought differently:

«As for my girl, I'm taking her! Let her answer for herself; I don't understand a thing about this.»

They all took advantage of this occasion to frighten us in every way they could. Next day, as we were passing by my uncle's house, my father had to wait a few minutes for my uncle. I ran to say goodbye to Jacinta, who was still in bed. Doubtful as to whether we would ever see one another again, I threw my arms around her. Bursting into tears, the poor child sobbed:

«If they kill you, tell them that Francisco and I are just the same as you, and that we want to die too. I'm going right now to the well with Francisco, and we'll pray hard for you.»

When I got back at nightfall, I ran to the well, and there were the pair of them on their knees, leaning over the side of the well, their heads buried in their hands, weeping bitterly. As soon as they saw me, they cried out in astonishment:

34

«You've come then? Why, your sister came here to draw water and told us that they'd killed you! We've been praying and crying so much for you!»

In Prison at Ourém

When, some time later, we were put in prison, what made Jacinta suffer most, was to feel that their parents had abandoned them. With tears streaming down her cheeks, she would say:

«Neither your parents nor mine have come to see us. They don't bother about us any more!»

«Don't cry,» said Francisco, «we can offer this to Jesus for sinners.»

Then, raising his eyes and hands to heaven, he made the offering:

«O my Jesus, this is for love of You, and for the conversion of sinners.»

Jacinta added:

«And also for the Holy Father, and in reparation for the sins committed against the Immaculate Heart of Mary.»

After being separated for awhile, we were re-united in one of the other rooms of the prison. When they told us they were coming soon to take us away to be fried alive, Jacinta went aside and stood by a window overlooking the cattle market. I thought at first that she was trying to distract her thoughts with the view, but I soon realized that she was crying. I went over and drew her close to me, asking her why she was crying:

«Because we are going to die,» she replied, «without ever seeing our parents again, not even our mothers!»

With tears running down her cheeks, she added:

«I would like at least to see my mother.»

«Don't you want, then, to offer this sacrifice for the conversion of sinners?»

«I do want to, I do!»

With her face bathed in tears, she joined her hands, raised her eyes to heaven and made her offering:

«O my Jesus! This is for love of You, for the conversion of sinners, for the Holy Father, and in reparation for the sins committed against the Immaculate Heart of Mary!»

The prisoners who were present at this scene, sought to console us:

«But all you have to do,» they said, «is to tell the Administrator the secret! What does it matter whether the Lady wants you to or not!»

«Never!» was Jacinta's vigorous reply, «I'd rather die.»

The Rosary in Jail

Next, we decided to say our Rosary. Jacinta took off a medal that she was wearing round her neck, and asked a prisoner to hang it up for her on a nail in the wall. Kneeling before this medal, we began to pray. The prisoners prayed with us, that is, if they knew how to pray, but at least they were down on their knees. Once the Rosary was over, Jacinta went over to the window, and started crying again.

«Jacinta,» I asked, «don't you want to offer this sacrifice to Our Lord?»

«Yes, I do, but I keep thinking about my mother, and I can't help crying.»

As the Blessed Virgin had told us to offer our prayers and sacrifices also in reparation for the sins committed against the Immaculate Heart of Mary, we agreed that each of us would choose one of these intentions. One would offer for sinners, another for the Holy Father and yet another in reparation for the sins against the Immaculate Heart of Mary. Having decided on this, I told Jacinta to choose whichever intention she preferred.

«I'm making the offering for all the intentions, because I love them all.»

And Finally... the Dance

Among the prisoners, there was one who played the concertina. To divert our attention, he began to play and they all started singing. They asked us if we knew how to dance. We said we knew the «fandango» and the «vira». Jacinta's partner was a poor thief who, finding her so tiny, picked her up and went on dancing with her in his arms! We only hope that Our Lady has had pity on his soul and converted him!

Now, Your Excellency will be saying: «What fine dispositions for martyrdom!» That is true. But we were only children and we didn't think beyond this. Jacinta dearly loved dancing, and had a special aptitude for it. I remember how she was crying one day about one of her brothers who had gone to the war and was reported killed in action. To distract her, I arranged a little dance with two of her brothers. There was the poor child dancing away as she dried the tears that ran down her cheeks. Her fondness for dancing was such, that the sound of some shepherd playing his instrument was enough to set her dancing all by herself. In spite of this, when Carnival time or St. John's Day festivities came round, she announced:

«I'm not going to dance any more.»

«And why not?»

«Because I want to offer this sacrifice to Our Lord.»

11. AFTER THE APPARITIONS

Prayers and Sacrifices at the Cabeço

My aunt was worn out with having continually to send someone to fetch her children, just to please the people who came asking to speak to them. She therefore handed over the care of the flock to her other son John. [15] This decision was very painful to Jacinta for two reasons: firstly, because she had to speak to everyone who came looking for her and, secondly, because she could no longer spend the whole day with me. She had to resign herself, however. To escape from the unwelcome visitors, she and Francisco used to go and hide in a cave hollowed out in the rock [16] on the hillside facing our hamlet. On top of the hill was a windmill. Situated as it is on the eastern slope, this hiding place is so well formed that it afforded them an ideal protection from both the rain and the burning sun, especially since it is sheltered by many oak and olive trees. How many were the prayers and sacrifices that Jacinta offered there to our dear Lord!

All over the slope grew innumerable varieties of flowers. Among them were many irises, and Jacinta loved these especially. Every evening she was waiting for me on my way home, holding an iris she had picked for me, or some other flower if there were no irises to be found. It was a real joy for her to pluck off the petals one by one, and strew them over me.

My mother was satisfied for the time being with deciding each day where I was to pasture the sheep, so that she knew where to find me when I was needed. When the place was nearby, I told my little companions, and they lost no time in coming out to join me. Jacinta never stopped running till she caught sight of me. Then, exhausted, she sat down and kept calling to me, until I answered and ran to meet her.

Troublesome Interrogations

Finally my mother, tired of seeing my sister waste her time coming to call me and taking my place with the sheep, decided to sell the lot. She talked things over with my aunt, and they agreed to send us off to school. At playtime, Jacinta loved to make a visit to the Blessed Sacrament.

«They seem to guess,» she complained. «We are no sooner inside the church than a crowd of people come asking us questions! I wanted so much to be alone for a long time with the Hidden Jesus and talk to Him, but they never let us.»

It was true, the simple country folk never left us alone. With the utmost simplicity, they told us all about their needs and their troubles. Jacinta showed the greatest compassion, especially when it concerned some sinner, saying: «We must pray and offer sacrifices to Our Lord, so that he will be converted and not go to hell, poor man!»

In this connection, it might be good to relate here an incident which shows to what extent Jacinta sought to escape from the people who came looking for her. We were on our way to Fatima one day, [17] and approaching the main road, when we noticed a group of ladies and gentlemen getting out of a car. We knew without the slightest doubt that they were looking for us. Escape was impossible, for they would see us. We continued on our way, hoping to pass by without being recognised. On reaching us, the ladies asked if we knew the little shepherds to whom Our Lady had appeared. We said we did.

«Do you know where they live?»

We gave them precise directions, and ran off to hide in the fields among the brambles. Jacinta was so delighted with the result of her little stratagem, that she exclaimed: «We must do this always when they don't know us by sight.»

The Saintly Father Cruz

One day, Father Cruz [18] from Lisbon came, in his turn, to question us. When he had finished, he asked us to show him the spot where Our Lady had appeared to us. On the way we walked on either side of His Reverence, who was riding a donkey so small that his feet almost touched the ground. As we went along, he taught us a litany of ejaculations, two of which Jacinta made her own and never stopped repeating ever afterwards: «O my Jesus, I love You! Sweet Heart of Mary, be my salvation!»

One day during her illness, she told me: «I so like to tell Jesus that I love Him! Many times, when I say it to Him, I seem to have a fire in my heart, but it doesn't burn me.»

Another time she said: «I love Our Lord and Our Lady so much, that I never get tired of telling them that I love them.»

Graces through Jacinta

There was a woman in our neighbourhood who insulted us every time we met her. We came upon her one day, as she was leaving a tavern, somewhat the worse for drink. Not satisfied with mere insults, she went still further. When she had finished, Jacinta said to me: «We have to plead with Our Lady and offer sacrifices for the conversion of this woman. She says so many sinful things that if she doesn't go to confession, she'll go to hell.»

A few days later, we were running past this woman's door when suddenly Jacinta stopped dead, and turning round, she asked:

«Listen! Is it tomorrow that we're going to see the Lady?»

«Yes, it is.»

«Then let's not play anymore. We can make this sacrifice for the conversion of sinners.»

Without realizing that some one might be watching her, she raised her hands and eyes to heaven, and made her offering. The woman, meanwhile, was peeping through a shutter in the house. She told my mother, afterwards, that what Jacinta did, made such an impression on her, that she needed no other proof to make her believe in the reality of the apparitions; henceforth, she would not only not insult us any more, but would constantly ask us to pray to Our Lady, that her sins might be forgiven.

Again, a poor woman afflicted with a terrible disease met us one day. Weeping, she knelt before Jacinta and begged her to ask Our Lady to cure her. Jacinta was distressed to see a woman kneeling before her, and caught hold of her with trembling hands to lift her up. But seeing this was beyond her strength, she, too, knelt down and said three Hail Marys with the woman. She then asked her to get up, and assured her that Our Lady would cure her. After that, she continued to pray daily for that woman, until she returned some time later, to thank Our Lady for her cure.

On another occasion, there was a soldier who wept like a child. He had been ordered to leave for the front, although his wife was sick in bed and he had three small children. He pleaded that either his wife would be cured or that the order would be revoked. Jacinta invited him to say the Rosary with her, and then said to him:

«Don't cry. Our Lady is so good! She will certainly grant you the grace you are asking.»

From then on, she never forgot her soldier. At the end of the Rosary, she always said one Hail Mary for him. Some months later, he appeared with his wife and his three small children, to thank Our Lady for the two graces he had received. Having gone down with fever on the eve of his departure, he had been released from military service, and as for his wife, he said she had been miraculously cured by Our Lady.

More and More Sacrifices

One day, we were told that a priest was coming to see us who was very holy and who could tell what was going on in people's inmost hearts. This meant that he would find out whether we were telling the truth or not. Full of joy, Jacinta exclaimed:

«When is this Father coming? If he can really tell, then he'll know we're telling the truth.»

We were playing one day at the well I have already mentioned. Close to it, there was a grape vine belonging to Jacinta's mother. She cut a few clusters and brought them to us to eat. But Jacinta never forgot her sinners.

«We won't eat them,» she said, «we'll offer this sacrifice for sinners.»

Then she ran out with the grapes and gave them to the other children playing on the road. She returned radiant with joy, for she had found our poor children, and given them the grapes.

Another time, my aunt called us to come and eat some figs which she had brought home, and indeed they would have given anybody an appetite. Jacinta sat down happily next to the basket, with the rest of us, and picked up the first fig. She was just about to eat it, when she suddenly remembered, and said:

«It's true! Today we haven't yet made a single sacrifice for sinners! We'll have to make this one.»

She put the fig back in the basket, and made the offering; and we, too, left our figs in the basket for the conversion of sinners. Jacinta made such sacrifices over and over again, but I won't stop to tell any more, or I shall never end.

111. ILLNESS AND DEATH OF JACINTA

Jacinta's Illness

This was how Jacinta spent her days, until Our Lord sent the influenza that confined her to bed, and her brother Francisco as well. [19] The evening before she fell sick, she said:

«I've a terrible headache and I'm so thirsty! But I won't take a drink, because I want to suffer for sinners.»

Apart from school or the small tasks I was given to do, I spent every free moment with my little companions. One day, when I called in on my way to school, Jacinta said to me:

«Listen! Tell the Hidden Jesus that I like Him very much, that I really love Him very much indeed.» At other times, she said:

«Tell Jesus that I send Him my love, and long to see Him.»

Whenever I visited her room first, she used to say: «Now go and see Francisco. I'll make the sacrifice of staying here alone.»

On another occasion, her mother brought her a cup of milk and told her to take it. «I don't want it, mother,» she answered, pushing the cup away with her little hand. My aunt insisted a little, and then left the room, saying: «I don't know how to make her take anything; she has no appetite.» As soon as we were alone, I asked her: «How can you disobey your mother like that, and not offer this sacrifice to Our Lord?» When she heard this, she shed a few tears

41

which I had the happiness of drying, and said: «I forgot this time.» She called her mother, asked her forgiveness, and said she'd take whatever she wanted. Her mother brought back the cup of milk, and Jacinta drank it down without the slightest sign of repugnance. Later, she told me:

«If you only knew how hard it was to drink that!»

Another time, she said to me: «It's becoming harder and harder for me to take milk and broth, but I don't say anything. I drink it all for love of Our Lord and of the Immaculate Heart of Mary, our dear heavenly Mother.»

Again, I asked her: «Are you better?»

«You know I'm not getting better,» she replied, and added: «I've such pains in my chest! But I don't say anything. I'm suffering for the conversion of sinners.»

One day when I arrived, she asked: «Did you make many sacrifices today? I've made a lot. My mother went out, and I wanted to go and visit Francisco many times, and I didn't go.»

Visit from the Blessed Virgin

Jacinta did improve somewhat, however. She was even able to get up, and could thus spend her days sitting on Francisco's bed. On one occasion, she sent for me to come and see her at once. I ran right over.

«Our Lady came to see us,» Jacinta said. «She told us she would come to take Francisco to heaven very soon, and she asked me if I still wanted to convert more sinners. I said I did. She told me I would be going to a hospital where I would suffer a great deal; and that I am to suffer for the conversion of sinners, in reparation for the sins committed against the Immaculate Heart of Mary, and for love of Jesus. I asked if you would go with me. She said you wouldn't, and that is what I find hardest. She said my mother would take me, and then I would have to stay there all alone!»

After this, she was thoughtful for awhile, and then added: «If only you could be with me! The hardest part is to go without you. Maybe, the hospital is a big dark house, where you can't see, and I'll be there suffering all alone! But never mind! I'll suffer for love of Our Lord, to make reparation to the Immaculate Heart of Mary, for the conversion of sinners and for the Holy Father.»

When the moment arrived for her brother to go to heaven, she confided to him these last messages: [20] «Give all my love to Our Lord and Our Lady, and tell them that I'll suffer as much as they want, for the conversion of sinners and in reparation to the Immaculate Heart of Mary.»

Jacinta suffered keenly when her brother died. She remained a long time buried in thought, and if anyone asked her what she was thinking about, she answered: «About Francisco. I'd give anything to see him again!» Then her eyes brimmed over with tears.

One day, I said to her: «It won't be long now till you go to heaven. But what about me!»

«You poor thing! Don't cry! I'll pray lots and lots for you when I'm there. As for you, that's the way Our Lady wants it. If she wanted that for me, I'd gladly stay and suffer more for sinners.»

In the Hospital at Ourém

The day came for Jacinta to go to hospital. [21] There indeed she was to suffer a great deal. When her mother went to see her, she asked if she wanted anything. She told her that she wanted to see me. This was no easy matter for my aunt, but she took me with her at the first opportunity. As soon as Jacinta saw me, she joyfully threw her arms around me, and asked her mother to leave me with her while she went to do her shopping. Then I asked her if she was suffering a lot.

«Yes, I am. But I offer everything for sinners, and in reparation to the Immaculate Heart of Mary.» Then, filled with enthusiasm, she spoke of Our Lord and Our Lady: «Oh, how much I love to suffer for love of Them, just to give Them pleasure! They greatly love those who suffer for the conversion of sinners.»

The time allotted for the visit passed rapidly, and my aunt arrived to take me home. She asked Jacinta if she wanted anything. The child begged her mother to bring me with her next time she came to see me. So my good aunt, who loved to make her little daughter happy, took me with her a second time. I found Jacinta as joyful as ever, glad to suffer for the love of our Good God and of the Immaculate Heart of Mary, for sinners and the Holy Father. That was her ideal, and she could speak of nothing else.

Return to Aljustrel

She returned home to her parents for yet a while. She had a large open wound in her chest which had to be treated every day, but she bore this without complaint and without the least sign of irritation. What distressed her most were the frequent visits and questionings on the part of many people who wanted to see her, and whom she could no longer avoid by running off to hide.

«I am offering this sacrifice too, for the conversion of sinners,» she said resignedly. «I would give anything to be able to go up to the Cabeço and say a Rosary there in our favourite place! But I am not able for it any more. When you go to the Cova da Iria pray for me. Just think, I shall never go there again!» The tears streamed down her cheeks.

One day my aunt made this request: «Ask Jacinta what she is thinking, when she covers her face with her hands and remains motionless for such a long while. I've already asked her, but she just smiles and does not answer.» I put the question to Jacinta.

«I think of Our Lord,» she replied, «of Our Lady, of sinners, and of... (and she mentioned certain parts of the Secret). I love to think.»

My aunt asked me how she answered. I just smiled. This led my aunt to tell my mother what had happened. «The life of these children is an enigma to me,» she exclaimed, «I can't understand it!» And my mother added: «Yes, and when they are alone, they talk nineteen to the dozen. Yet, however hard you listen, you can never catch a single word! I just can't understand all this mystery.»

Renewed Visits from the Blessed Virgin

Once again, the Blessed Virgin deigned to visit Jacinta, to tell her of new crosses and sacrifices awaiting her. She gave me the news saying:

«She told me that I am going to Lisbon to another hospital; that I will not see you again, nor my parents either, and after suffering a great deal, I shall die alone. But she said I must not be afraid, since she herself is coming to take me to heaven.»

She hugged me and wept: «I will never see you again!

You won't be coming to visit me there. Oh please, pray hard for me, because I am going to die alone!»

Jacinta suffered terribly right up until the day of her departure for Lisbon. She kept clinging to me and sobbing: «I'll never see you again! Nor my mother, nor my brothers, nor my father! I'll never see anybody ever again! And then, I'll die all alone!»

«Don't think about it,» I advised her one day.

«Let me think about it,» she replied, «for the more I think the more I suffer, and I want to suffer for love of Our Lord and for sinners. Anyway, I don't mind! Our Lady will come to me there and take me to heaven.»

At times, she kissed and embraced a crucifix, exclaiming: «O my Jesus! I love You, and I want to suffer very much for love of You.» How often did she say: «O Jesus! Now You can convert many sinners, because this is really a big sacrifice!»

From time to time, she asked me: «Am I going to die without receiving the Hidden Jesus? If only Our Lady would bring Him to me, when she comes to fetch me!»

One day I asked her: «What are you going to do in heaven?»

«I'm going to love Jesus very much, and the Immaculate Heart of Mary, too. I'm going to pray a lot for you, for sinners, for the Holy Father, for my parents and my brothers and sisters, and for all the people who have asked me to pray for them...»

When her mother looked sad at seeing the child so ill, Jacinta used to say:

«Don't worry, mother. I'm going to heaven, and there I'll be praying so much for you.»

Or again: «Don't cry. I'm alright.» If they asked her if she needed anything, she answered: «No, I don't, thank you.» Then when they had left the room, she said: «I'm so thirsty, but I don't want to take a drink. I'm offering it to Jesus for sinners.»

One day, when my aunt had been asking me many questions, Jacinta called me to her and said: «I don't want you to tell anybody that I'm suffering, not even my mother; I do not want to upset her.»

On one occasion, I found her clasping a picture of Our Lady to her heart, and saying, «O my dearest heavenly Mother, do I have to die all alone?» The poor child seemed so frightened at the thought of dying alone! I tried to comfort her, saying: «What does it matter if you die alone, so long as Our Lady is coming to fetch you?»

«It's true, it doesn't matter, really. I don't know why it is, but I sometimes forget Our Lady is coming to take me. I only remember that I'll die without having you near me.»

Leaving for Lisbon

The day came [22] at last when she was to leave for Lisbon. It was a heartrending farewell. For a long time, she clung to me with her arms around my neck, and sobbed: «We shall never see each other again! Pray a lot for me, until I go to heaven. Then I will pray a lot for you. Never tell the Secret to anyone, even if they kill you. Love Jesus and the Immaculate Heart of Mary very much, and make many sacrifices for sinners.»

From Lisbon, she sent me word that Our Lady had come to see her there; she had told her the day and hour of her death. Finally Jacinta reminded me to be very good.

EPILOGUE

And now, I have finished telling Your Excellency what I remember about Jacinta's life. I ask our Good God to deign to accept this act of obedience, that it may kindle in souls a fire of love for the Hearts of Jesus and Mary.

I would like to ask just one favour. If Your Excellency should publish anything [23] of what I have just written, would you do it in such a way that no mention whatsoever is made of my poor and miserable self. I must confess, moreover, that if it were to come to my knowledge that Your Excellency had burnt this account, without even reading it, I would be very glad indeed, since I wrote it solely out of obedience to the will of our Good God, as made known to me through the express will of Your Excellency.

NOTES: FIRST MEMOIR

1. Dom José Alves Correia da Silva, 1872-1957, first Bishop of the re-established Diocese of Leiria to which Fatima belongs.
2. Luke 2, 19.51.
3. Fr. António de Oliveira Reis, died 1962, at that time Vicar of Torres Novas.
4. Fr. Faustino José Jacinto Ferreira, died 1924.
5. Despite her inadequate schooling, Lucia had quite a talent for poetry, and wrote various poems.
6. Maria dos Anjos, Lucia's eldest sister, who now, in 1976, is 85 years of age.
7. Visitors can still see this Crucifix at Lucia's old home.
8. Carolina is married and is still living in Casa Velha near Aljustrel.
9. Jacinta was born on the 11th of March, 1910.
10. A small hamlet, north of the Cova da Iria where the Apparitions took place.
11. The first interrogation by the parish priest took place at the end of May, 1917.
12. On May 13th, 1967, Pope Paul VI visited the Sanctuary of Fatima as a pilgrim.
13. Her father's name was António dos Santos, died 1919. Her uncle was Manuel Pedro Marto, died 1957, father of Francisco and Jacinta.
14. The Administrator was Arturo de Oliveira Santos, died 1955.
15. John Marto, Jacinta's brother, is still living in the old home.
16. The hill is called the «Cabeço», and the cave on its slope is known as «Loca do Cabeço».
17. This happened in the course of 1918-1919, one year after the Apparitions.
18. Fr. Francisco Cruz, S. J., 1859-1948, Servant of God, whose Cause of Beatification has been instituted.
19. Jacinta fell ill in October, 1918, and Francisco soon after.
20. Francisco died on April 4th, 1919.
21. This was St. Augustine's Hospital in Vila Nova de Ourém. She was taken there on July lst and left it on August 31st, 1919.
22. On January 21st, 1920, she was taken to Lisbon, where she was admitted to the Orphanage run by Madre Godinho, Rua da Estrela, 17. On February 2nd, she was taken to the Dona Estefânia Hospital, where she died on February 20th, 1920, at 10.30 p.m.
23. Lucia's reminiscences in this first Memoir were used by Dr. José Galamba de Oliveira for his book «Jacinta, the Flower of Fatima» (May 1938).

SECOND MEMOIR

Introduction

The first manuscript of Lucia's Memoirs made it clear to her Superiors that she was still jealously guarding quite a number of things which she would probably reveal only under obedience. In April, 1937, Fr. Fonseca wrote to the Bishop: «...The Second Memoir makes one think that there are further interesting details in the history of the Apparitions... which are not yet known. Would it not be possible, or would there be any difficulty in persuading Sister Lucia to write down in detail, conscientiously and with the simplicity of the Gospel, and in honour of the Blessed Virgin, every single thing she still remembers? This is an idea, and should you find it helpful, only Your Excellency can put it into effect...»

In agreement with the Mother Provincial of the Dorothean Sisters, Madre Maria do Carmo Corte Real, Bishop José gave Lucia the necessary order. In reply, she wrote to the Bishop on November 7th, 1937: «I have already begun today, for this is the Will of God.» Thus, this manuscript was started on November 7th, and finished, as we know, on the 21st... That means it took her only a fortnight to compose such a long document. Besides, she was frequently interrupted by housework, which did not allow her any free time. As already mentioned, the document consisted of 38 pages, filled front and back with close handwriting, almost without corrections. Once again, we see how this reveals Sister Lucia's clear mind, her composure and her mental equilibrium.

The subjects dealt with in this Memoir are even more surprising: angelic apparitions, extraordinary blessings on the occasion of her First Communion, the Immaculate Heart of Mary in the Apparition of June, 1917, and many other details totally unknown until then.

What Sister Lucia intended when she wrote this account is explained by her as revealing «the story of Fatima just as it is». Therefore, it was not a question of a few biographical data as in the previous Memoir, where the subject of the Apparitions was kept in the background. In the present Memoir, the Apparitions themselves are given more prominence.

The spirit in which Lucia wrote can be gathered from the words: «No longer will I savour the joy of sharing with You alone the secrets of Your love, but henceforth, others too, will sing the greatness of Your mercy... Behold the handmaid of the Lord! May He continue to make use of her, as He thinks best.»

J. M. J.

O Will of God, You are my Paradise. [1]

FOREWORD

Your Excellency,

Here I am, pen in hand, ready to do the will of my God. Since I have no other aim but this, I begin with the maxim which my holy Foundress has handed down to me, and which, after her example, I shall repeat many times in the course of this account: «O Will of God, you are my paradise!»

Allow me, Your Excellency, to sound the depths contained in this maxim. Whenever repugnance or love for my secret makes me want to keep some things hidden, then this maxim will be my norm and my guide.

I had a mind to ask what use there could possibly be in my writing an account like this, since even my hand-writing is scarcely presentable. [2] But I am asking nothing. I know that the perfection of obedience asks for no reasons. Your Excellency's words are enough for me, since they assure me that this is for the glory of our Blessed Mother in heaven. In the certainty that it is so, I implore the blessing and protection of her Immaculate Heart and, humbly prostrate at her feet, I use her own most holy words to speak to my God:

«I, the least of your handmaids, O my God, now come in full submission to your most holy Will, to lift the veil from my secret, and reveal the story of Fatima just as it is. No longer will I savour the joy of sharing with You alone the secrets of Your love; but henceforth, others too, will sing with me the greatness of Your mercy!»

1. BEFORE THE APPARITIONS

Lucia's Childhood

Your Excellency,

«The Lord has looked upon His lowly handmaid»: that is why all peoples will sing the greatness of His mercy. [3]

It seems to me, Your Excellency, that our dear Lord deigned to favour me with the use of reason from my earliest childhood. I remember being conscious of my actions, even from my mother's arms. I remember being rocked, and falling asleep to the sound of lullabies. Our Lord blessed my parents with five girls and one boy, [4] [5] of whom I was the youngest, [6] and I remember how they used to squabble, because they all wanted to hold me in their arms and play with me. On such occasions none of them ever succeeded, because my mother used to take me away from them altogether. If she was too busy to hold me herself, she would give me to my father, and he also would fondle me and cover me with caresses.

The first thing I learned was the Hail Mary. While holding me in her arms, my mother taught it to my sister Carolina, the second youngest, and five years older than myself. My two eldest sisters were already grown up. My mother, knowing that I repeated everything I heard like a parrot, wanted them to take me with them everywhere they went. They were, as we say in our locality, the leading lights among the young people. There was not a festival or a dance that they did not attend. At Carnival time, on St. John's Day and at Christmas, there was certain to be a dance.

Besides this, there was the vintage. Then there was the olive picking, with a dance almost every day. When the big parish festivals came round, such as the feasts of the Sacred Heart of Jesus, Our Lady of the Rosary, St. Anthony, and so on, we always raffled cakes; after that came a dance, without fail. We were invited to almost all the weddings for miles around, for if they did not invite my mother to be matron of honour, they were sure to need her for the cooking. At these weddings, the dancing went on from after the banquet until well into the next morning. Since my sisters had to have me always with them, they took as much trouble in dressing me up as they were wont to do for themselves. As one of them was a dressmaker, I was always decked out in a regional costume more elegant than that of any other girl around. I wore a pleated skirt, a shiny belt, a cashmere kerchief with the corners hanging down behind, and a hat decorated with gold beads and bright coloured feathers. You would have thought sometimes, that they were dressing a doll rather than a small child.

Popular Entertainments

At the dances, they deposited me on top of a wooden chest or some other tall piece of furniture, to save me from being trampled underfoot. Once on my perch, I had to sing a number of songs to the music of the guitar or the concertina. My sisters had already taught me to sing, as well as to dance a few waltzes when there was a partner missing. The latter I performed with rare skill, thus attracting the attention and applause of everyone present. Some of them even rewarded me with gifts, in the hope of pleasing my sisters.

On Sunday afternoons, all these young people used to gather in our yard, in the shade of three large figtrees in summer, and in winter in an open porch that we had where my sister Maria's house now stands. There they spent the afternoons, playing and chatting with my sisters. It was there that we used to raffle the sugared almonds at Easter time, and most of them usually found their way into my pocket, as some of the winners hoped thereby to gain our good graces. My mother would spend these afternoons seated at the kitchen door looking out on the yard, so that she could see all that was going on. Sometimes she held a book in her hand and would read for awhile; at other times, she chatted with my aunts or neighbours, who sat beside her. She was always very serious, and everybody knew that what she said was like Scripture and must be obeyed without more ado. I never knew anyone to say a disrespectful word in her presence, or show her any lack of consideration. It was the general opinion among them, that my mother was worth more than all her daughters put together. I often heard my mother say:

«I don't know how those people enjoy running about chattering from house to house! As for me, there's nothing as good as just staying at home for a nice quiet read! These books are full of such wonderful things! And as for the lives of the saints, they're simply beautiful!»

It seems to me that I have already told Your Excellency how, during the week, I used to spend the day surrounded by a crowd of children from the neighbourhood. Their mothers went out to work in the fields, so they used to ask my mother if they could leave the children with me. When I wrote to Your Excellency about my cousin, I think I also described our games and amusements, so I will not dwell on them here.

Amid the warmth of such affectionate and tender caresses, I happily spent my first six years. To tell the truth, the world was beginning to smile on me, and above all, a passion for dancing was already sinking its roots deep into my poor heart. And I must confess that the devil would have used this to bring about my ruin, had not the good Lord shown His special mercy towards me.

If I am not mistaken, I have also told Your Excellency in the same account, how my mother was accustomed to teach catechism to her children during the summer at siesta time. In the winter, we had our lesson after supper at night, gathered round the fireside, as we sat roasting and eating chestnuts and a sweet variety of acorns.

Lucia's First Communion

The day which the parish priest had appointed for the solemn First Communion of the children of the parish, was drawing near. In view of the fact that I knew my catechism and was already six years old, my mother thought that perhaps I could now make my First Communion. To this end, she sent me with my sister Carolina to the catechism instructions which the parish priest was giving to the children, in preparation for this great day. I went, therefore, radiant with joy, hoping soon to be able to receive my God for the first time. The priest gave his instructions, seated in a chair up on a platform. He called me to his side, and when one or other of the children was unable to answer his questions, he told me to give the answer instead, just to shame them.

The eve of the great day arrived, and the priest sent word that all the children were to go to the church in the forenoon, so that he could make the final decision as to which ones were to receive their First Communion. What was not my disappointment when he called me up beside him, caressed me and then said I was to wait till I was seven old! I began to cry at once, and just as I would have done with my own mother, I laid my head on his knees and sobbed. It happened that another priest [7] who had been called in to help with the confessions, entered the church just at that moment. Seeing me in this position, he asked the reason for my tears. On being informed, he took me along to the sacristy and examined me on the catechism and the mystery

53

of the Eucharist. After this, he took me by the hand and brought me to the parish priest, saying:

«Father Pena, you can let this child go to Communion. She understands what she's doing better than many of the others.»

«But she's only six years old,» objected the good priest.

«Never mind! I'll take the responsibility for that.»

«Alright then,» the good priest said to me. «Go and tell your mother that you are making your First Communion tomorrow.»

I could never express the joy I felt. Off I went, clapping my hands with delight, and running all the way home to give the good news to my mother. She at once set about preparing me for the Confession I was to make that afternoon. My mother took me to the church, and when we arrived, I told her that I wanted to confess to the other priest. So we went to the sacristy, where he was sitting on a chair hearing confessions. My mother knelt down in front of the high altar near the sacristy door, together with the other mothers who were waiting for their children to confess in turn. Right there before the Blessed Sacrament, my mother gave me her last recommendations.

Our Lady of the Rosary Smiles at Lucia

When my turn came round, I went and knelt at the feet of our dear Lord, represented there in the person of His minister, imploring forgiveness for my sins. When I had finished, I noticed that everyone was laughing.

My mother called me to her and said: «My child, don't you know that confession is a secret matter and that it is made in a low voice? Everybody heard you! There was only one thing nobody heard: that is what you said at the end.»

On the way home, my mother made several attempts to discover what she called the secret of my confession. But the only answer she obtained was complete silence.

Now, however, I am going to reveal the secret of my first confession. After listening to me, the good priest said these few words:

«My child, your soul is the temple of the Holy Spirit. Keep it always pure, so that He will be able to carry on His divine action within it.»

On hearing these words, I felt myself filled with respect for my interior, and asked the kind confessor what I ought to do.

«Kneel down there before Our Lady and ask her, with great confidence, to take care of your heart, to prepare it to receive Her beloved Son worthily tomorrow, and to keep it for Him alone!»

In the Church, there was more than one statue of Our Lady; but as my sisters took care of the altar of Our Lady of the Rosary, [8] I usually went there to pray. That is why I went there on this occasion also, to ask her with all the ardour of my soul, to keep my poor heart for God alone. As I repeated this humble prayer over and over again, with my eyes fixed on the statue, it seemed to me that she smiled and, with a loving look and kindly gesture, assured me that she would. My heart was overflowing with joy, and I could scarcely utter a single word.

Eager Expectancy

My sisters stayed up that night making me a white dress and a wreath of flowers. As for me, I was so happy that I could not sleep, and it seemed as if the hours would never pass! I kept on getting up to ask them if the day had come, or if they wanted me to try on my dress, or my wreath, and so forth.

The happy day dawned at last; but nine o'clock — how long it was in coming! I put on my white dress, and then my sister Maria took me into the kitchen to ask pardon of my parents, to kiss their hands and ask their blessing. After this little ceremony, my mother gave me her last recommendations. She told me what she wanted me to ask Our Lord when I had received Him into my heart, and said goodbye to me in these words:

«Above all, ask Him to make you a saint.»

Her words made such an indelible impression on my heart, that they were the very first that I said to Our Lord when I received Him. Even today, I seem to hear the echo of my mother's voice repeating these words to me. I set out for the church with my sisters, and my brother carried me all the way in his arms, so that not a speck of dust from the road would touch me. As soon as I arrived at the church, I ran to kneel before the altar of Our Lady to renew my petition. There I remained in contemplation of Our Lady's smile of the previous day, until my sisters came in search of me and took me to my appointed place. There was a large number of children, arranged in four lines — two of boys and two of girls — from the back of the church right up to the altar rails. Being the smallest, it happened that I was the one nearest to the «angels» on the step by the altar rails.

The Great Day

Once the Missa Cantata began and the great moment drew near, my heart beat faster and faster, in expectation of the visit of the great God who was about to descend from heaven, to unite Himself to my poor soul. The parish priest came down and passed among the rows of children, distributing the Bread of Angels. I had the good fortune to be the first one to receive. As the priest was coming down the altar steps, I felt as though my heart would leap from my breast. But he had no sooner placed the Divine Host on my tongue than I felt an unalterable serenity and peace. I felt myself bathed in such a supernatural atmosphere that the presence of our dear Lord became as clearly perceptible to me as if I had seen and heard Him with my bodily senses. I then addressed my prayer to Him:

«O Lord, make me a saint. Keep my heart always pure, for You alone.»

Then it seemed that in the depths of my heart, our dear Lord distinctly spoke these words to me:

«The grace granted to you this day will remain living in your soul, producing fruits of eternal life.»

I felt as though transformed in God.

It was almost one o'clock before the ceremonies were over, on account of the late arrival of priests coming from a distance, the sermon and the renewal of baptismal promises. My mother came looking for me, quite distressed, thinking I might faint from weakness. But I, filled to overflowing with the Bread of Angels, found it impossible to take any food whatsoever. After this, I lost the taste and attraction for the things of the world, and only felt at home in some solitary place where, all alone, I could recall the delights of my First Communion.

Lucia's Family

Such moments of seclusion were rare indeed. As Your Excellency already knows, I had to look after the children whom the neighbours entrusted to our care; and besides this, my mother was in much demand thereabouts as a nurse. In cases of minor ills, people came to our house to seek her advice, but when the sick person was unable to go out, they asked my mother to go to their homes. She often spent entire days there, and even nights. If the illness was prolonged, or the sick person's condition required it, she occasionally sent my sisters to stay by the patient's bedside at night, to give the family a chance to get some rest. Whenever the sick person was the mother of a young family, or some one who could not stand the noise of children, my mother brought the little ones to our house and charged me with keeping them occupied. I kept the children amused, by teaching them how to prepare the yarn for weaving: they set the wooden winder spinning to wind it into balls; they rolled it into spools; they strung it on the skeiner to make it into skeins; and they guided the balls of yarn as the warp was prepared on the frame.

In this way, we always had plenty to do. There were usually several girls working in our house, who had come to learn weaving and dress-making. Normally, these girls showed great affection for our family, and used to say that the best days of their lives were those spent in our house. At certain times of the year, my sisters had to go out working in the fields during the daytime, so they did their weaving and sewing at night. Supper was followed by prayers led by my father, [9] and then the work began.

Everyone had something to do: My sister Maria went to the loom; my father filled the spools; Teresa and Gloria went to their sewing; my mother took up her spinning; Carolina and I, after tidying up the kitchen, had to help with the sewing, taking out basting, sewing on buttons, and so forth; to keep drowsiness away, my brother played the concertina, and we joined in singing all kinds of songs. The neighbours often dropped in to keep us company; and although it meant losing their sleep, they used to tell us that the very sound of our gaiety banished all their worries and filled them with happiness. I heard different women sometimes say to my mother:

«How fortunate you are! What lovely children God has given you!»

When the time came round to harvest the corn, we removed the husks by moonlight. There was I sitting atop a heap of corn, and chosen to give a hug all round whenever a dark-coloured corn cob appeared.

In Retrospect

I don't know whether the facts I have related above about my First Communion were a reality or a little child's illusion. What I do know is that they always had, and still have today, a great influence in uniting me to God. What I don't know either is why I am telling Your Excellency all this about our family life. But it is God who inspires me to do so, and He knows the reason for it. Perhaps it is to let you see how, after having had so much affection lavished upon me, I would feel all the more deeply the suffering our dear Lord was going to ask of me. As Your Excellency has told me to give an account of all the sufferings that Our Lord has sent me, and all the graces which He has deigned, in His mercy, to grant me, I think it best to tell them just as they actually happened. [10] Moreover, I feel quite at peace about it, because I know Your Excellency will put into the fire whatever you see does not further the glory of God and of Mary most Holy.

2. THE APPARITIONS

Lucia the Shepherdess

This was how things were until I was seven years old. My mother then decided that I should take over the care of our sheep. My father did not agree, nor did my sisters. They were so fond of me, that they wanted an exception made in my case. My mother would not give in. «She's just like the rest,» she said, «Carolina is already twelve years old. That means she can now begin to work in the fields, or else, learn to be a weaver or a seamstress, whichever she prefers.»

The care of our flock was then given to me. [11] News that I was beginning my life as a shepherdess spread rapidly among the other shepherds; almost all of them came and offered to be my companions. I said «Yes» to everybody, and arranged with each one to meet on the slopes of the serra. Next day, the serra was a solid mass of sheep with their shepherds, as though a cloud had descended upon it. But I felt ill at ease in the midst of such a hubbub. I therefore chose three companions from among the shepherds, and without saying a word to anyone, we arranged to pasture our sheep on the opposite slopes. These were the three I chose: Teresa Matias, her sister Maria Rosa and Maria Justino. [12] On the following day, we set out in the direction of a hill known as the Cabeço. We went up the northern slope. Valinhos, a place that Your Excellency already knows by name, is on the southern side of the same hill. On the eastern slope is the cave I have already spoken of, in my account of Jacinta. Together with our flocks, we climbed almost to the top of the hill. At our feet lay a wide expanse of trees — olives, oaks, pines, holmoaks, and so on, that stretched away down towards the level valley below.

A Mysterious Presage in 1915

Around midday, we ate our lunch. After this, I invited my companions to pray the Rosary with me, to which they eagerly agreed. We had hardly begun when, there before our eyes, we saw a figure poised in the air above the trees; it looked like a statue made of snow, rendered almost transparent by the rays of the sun.

«What is that?» asked my companions, quite frightened.

«I don't know!»

We went on praying, with our eyes fixed on the figure before us, and as we finished our prayer, the figure disappeared. As was usual with me, I resolved to say nothing; but my companions told their families what had happened the very moment they reached home. The news soon spread, and one day when I arrived home, my mother questioned me:

«Look here! They say you've seen I don't know what, up there. What was it you saw?»

«I don't know,» and as I could not explain it myself, I went on:

«It looked like a person wrapped up in a sheet!» As I meant to say that I couldn't discern its features, I added:

«You couldn't make out any eyes, or hands, on it.»

My mother put an end to the whole matter with a gesture of disgust: «Childish nonsense!» [13]

After some time, we returned with our flocks to the same place, and the very same thing happened again. My companions once more told the whole story. After a brief interval, the same thing was repeated. It was the third time that my mother heard all these things being talked about outside, without my having said a single word about them at home. She called me, therefore, quite displeased, and demanded:

«Now, let us see! What is it that you girls say you saw over there?»

«I don't know, Mother. I don't know what it is!»

Some people started making fun of us. My sisters, recalling that for some time after my First Communion I had been quite abstracted, used to ask me rather scornfully:

«Do you see someone wrapped in a sheet?»

I felt these contemptuous words and gestures very keenly, as up to now I had been used to nothing but caresses. But this was nothing, really. You see, I did not know what the good Lord had in store for me in the future.

Apparitions of the Angel in 1916

Around this time, as I have already related to Your Excellency, Francisco and Jacinta sought and obtained permission from their parents to start taking care of their own flock. So I left my good companions, and I joined my cousins, Francisco and Jacinta, instead. To avoid going to the serra with all the other shepherds, we arranged to pasture our flocks on properties belonging to my uncle and aunt and my parents.

One fine day, we set out with our sheep for some land that my parents owned, which lay at the foot of the eastern slope of the hill that I have already mentioned. This property was called Chousa Velha. Soon after our arrival, about mid-morning, a fine drizzle began to fall, so fine that it seemed like mist. We went up the hillside, followed by our flocks, looking for an overhanging boulder where we could take shelter. Thus it was for the first time that we entered this blessed hollow among the rocks. It stood in the middle of an olive grove belonging to my godfather Anastácio. From there, you could see the little village where I was born, my parents' home, and the hamlets of Casa Velha and Eira da Pedra.

...mente ao Altíssimo, orações e sacrifícios. Como nos havemos de sacrificar? (perguntei) De tudo que poderdes oferece a Deus sacrifício em acto de reparação pelos pecados com que Ele é ofendido e súplica pela conversão dos pecadores; atrai assim sôbre a vossa Pátria a paz; eu sou o Anjo da sua Guarda, o Anjo de Portugal. Sobre tudo aceitai e suportai com submissão o sofrimento que o Senhor vos enviar.

Tornou-se bastante tarde e fomos pastorar os nossos rebanhos para uma propriedade de meus Pais que fica na encosta do já mencionado monte um pouco mais a cima, e uma olival a que chamávamos pregueira.

Depois de termos merendado combinámos ir rezar na gruta que ficava ao outro lado do monte, demos para isso uma volta pela encosta e tivemos que subir uns rochedos que ficam a cimo da pregueira; as ovelhas conseguiram passar com muita dificuldade, logo que aí chegámos de joelhos com os rostos em terra começamos a repetir a oração do Anjo. Meu Deus! Eu creio, Adoro, Espero e Amo-vos etc. Não sei quantas vezes tinhamos repetido esta oração, quando vemos que sôbre nós brilha uma luz desconhecida; erguemo-nos para ver o que se passava, e vemos o Anjo tendo em a mão esquerda um cális sôbre o qual está suspensa uma Hóstia da qual caem algumas gotas de sangue dentro do

The olive grove, owned by several people, extended to within the confines of the hamlets themselves. We spent the day there among the rocks, in spite of the fact that the rain was over and the sun was shining bright and clear. We ate our lunch and said our Rosary. I'm not sure whether we said it that day in the way I have already described to Your Excellency, saying just the word Hail-Mary and Our-Father on each bead, so great was our eagerness to get to our play! Our prayer finished, we started to play «pebbles»!

We had enjoyed the game for a few moments only, when a strong wind began to shake the trees. We looked up, startled, to see what was happening, for the day was unusually calm. Then we saw coming towards us, above the olive trees, the figure I have already spoken about. [14] Jacinta and Francisco had never seen it before, nor had I ever mentioned it to them. As it drew closer, we were able to distinguish its features. It was a young man, about fourteen or fifteen years old, whiter than snow, transparent as crystal when the sun shines through it, and of great beauty. On reaching us, he said:

«Do not be afraid! I am the Angel of Peace. Pray with me.»

Kneeling on the ground, he bowed down until his forehead touched the ground, and made us repeat these words three times:

«My God, I believe, I adore, I hope and I love You! I ask pardon of You for those who do not believe, do not adore, do not hope and do not love You.»

Then, rising, he said: «Pray thus. The Hearts of Jesus and Mary are attentive to the voice of your supplications.»

His words engraved themselves so deeply on our minds that we could never forget them. From then on, we used to spend long periods of time, prostrate like the Angel, repeating his words, until sometimes we fell, exhausted. I warned my companions, right away, that this must be kept secret and, thank God, they did what I wanted.

Some time passed, [15] and summer came, when we had to go home for siesta. One day, we were playing on the stone slabs of the well down at the bottom of the garden belonging to my parents, which we called the Arneiro. (I have already mentioned this well to Your Excellency in my account of Jacinta). Suddenly, we saw beside us the same figure, or rather Angel, as it seemed to me.

cáliz. O Anjo deixa suspenso no ar o cáliz, aquella junto de nós, e faz-nos repetir tres vezes: Santíssima Trindade: Padre Filho Espírito Santo, ofereço-vos o preciosíssimo Corpo Sangue, Alma e Divindade de Jesus Cristo, presente em todos os Sacrários da terra, em reparação dos ultrages, sacrilégios e indiferenças com que Ele mesmo é ofendido, e pelos méritos infinitos do seu Santíssimo Coração e do Coração Imaculado de Maria, peço-vos a conversão dos pobres pecadores. Depois levanta-se toma em suas mãos o Cáliz e a Hóstia; dá-me a Sagrada Hóstia a mim e o sangue do Cáliz dividiu pela Jacinta e o Francisco, dizendo ao mesmo tempo: Tomai e bebei o Corpo e Sangue de Jesus Cristo, orrivelmente ultrajado pelos homens ingratos; reparai os seus crimes e consolai o vosso Deus, e prostrando-se de novo em terra repetiu-conosco outras tres vezes a mesma oração Santíssima Trindade etc. e desaparece, nós permanecemos na mesma atitude repetindo sempre as mesmas palavras e quando nos erguemos vimos que era noite e por isso horas de virmos para casa. Eis-eu chegado Ex.mo e Rev.mo Senhor ao fim dos meus tres anos de pastorinha dos 7 aos 15, durante estes tres anos a nossa casa e quaisi me atrevia a dizer a nossa freguezia tinha mudado quaisi completamente

«What are you doing?» he asked. «Pray, pray very much! The most holy Hearts of Jesus and Mary have designs of mercy on you. Offer prayers and sacrifices constantly to the Most High.»

«How are we to make sacrifices?» I asked.

«Make of everything you can a sacrifice, and offer it to God as an act of reparation for the sins by which He is offended, and in supplication for the conversion of sinners. You will thus draw down peace upon your country. I am its Angel Guardian, the Angel of Portugal. Above all, accept and bear with submission, the suffering which the Lord will send you.»

A considerable time had elapsed, when one day we went to pasture our sheep on a property belonging to my parents, which lay on the slope of the hill I have mentioned, a little higher up than Valinhos. It is an olive grove called Pregueira. After our lunch, we decided to go and pray in the hollow among the rocks on the opposite side of the hill. To get there, we went around the slope, and had to climb over some rocks above the Pregueira. The sheep could only scramble over these rocks with great difficulty.

As soon as we arrived there, we knelt down, with our foreheads touching the ground, and began to repeat the prayer of the Angel:

«My God, I believe, I adore, I hope and I love You...» I don't know how many times we had repeated this prayer, when an extraordinary light shone upon us. We sprang up to see what was happening, and beheld the Angel. He was holding a chalice in his left hand, with the Host suspended above it, from which some drops of blood fell into the chalice. [16] Leaving the chalice suspended in the air, the Angel knelt down beside us and made us repeat three times:

«Most Holy Trinity, Father, Son and Holy Spirit, I offer You the most precious Body, Blood, Soul and Divinity of Jesus Christ, present in all the tabernacles of the world, in reparation for the outrages, sacrileges and indifference with which He Himself is offended. And, through the infinite merits of His most Sacred Heart, and the Immaculate Heart of Mary, I beg of You the conversion of poor sinners.» [17]

Then, rising, he took the chalice and the Host in his hands. He gave the Sacred Host to me, and shared the Blood from the chalice between Jacinta and Francisco, [18] saying as he did so:

«Take and drink the Body and Blood of Jesus Christ, horribly outraged by ungrateful men! Make reparation for their crimes and console your God.»

Once again, he prostrated on the ground and repeated with us, three times more, the same prayer «Most Holy Trinity...», and then disappeared.

We remained a long time in this position, repeating the same words over and over again. When at last we stood up, we noticed that it was already dark, and therefore time to return home.

Trouble at Home

Here I am, Your Excellency, at the end of my three years as a shepherdess, from the time I was seven until I was ten years old. During these three years, our home, and I would venture to say, our parish as well, underwent an almost total change. Reverend Father Pena was no longer our parish priest, and had been replaced by Reverend Father Boicinha. [19] When this most zealous priest learned that such a pagan custom as endless dancing was only too common in the parish, he promptly began to preach against it from the pulpit in his Sunday sermons. In public and in private, he lost no opportunity of attacking this bad custom. As soon as my mother heard the good priest speak in this fashion, she forbade my sisters to attend such amusements. As my sisters' example led others also to refrain from attending, this custom gradually died out. The same thing happened among the children, who used to get up their little dances apart, as I have already explained to Your Excellency when writing about my cousin Jacinta.

Apropos of this, somebody remarked one day to my mother: «Up to now, it was no sin to go to dances, but just because we have a new parish priest, it is a sin. How could that be?»

«I don't know,» replied my mother. «All I know is that the priest does not want dancing, so my daughters are not going to such gatherings any more. At most, I would let them dance a bit within the family, because the priest says there is no harm in that.»

During this period, my two eldest sisters left home, after receiving the sacrament of matrimony. My father had fallen into bad company, and let his weakness get the better of him; this meant the loss of some of our property. [20] When my mother realized that our means of livelihood were diminishing, she resolved to send my two sisters, Gloria and Carolina, out to work as servants.

At home, there remained only my brother, to look after our few remaining fields; my mother, to take care of the house; and myself, to take our sheep out to pasture. My poor mother seemed just drowned in the depths of distress. When we gathered round the fire at night time, waiting for my father to come in to supper, my mother would look at her daughters' empty places and exclaim with profound sadness: «My God, where has all the joy of our home gone?» Then, resting her head on a little table beside her, she would burst into bitter tears. My brother and I wept with her. It was one of the saddest scenes I have ever witnessed. What with longing for my sisters, and seeing my mother so miserable, I felt my heart was just breaking. Although I was only a child, I understood perfectly the situation we were in.

Then I remembered the Angel's words: «Above all, accept submissively the sacrifices that the Lord will send you.» At such times, I used to withdraw to a solitary place, so as not to add to my mother's suffering, by letting her see my own. This place, usually, was our well. There, on my knees, leaning over the edge of the stone slabs that covered the well, my tears mingled with the waters below and I offered my suffering to God. Sometimes, Jacinta and Francisco would come and find me like this, in bitter grief. As my voice was choked with sobs and I couldn't say a word, they shared my suffering to such a degree that they also wept copious tears. Then Jacinta made our offering aloud: «My God, it is as an act of reparation, and for the conversion of sinners, that we offer You all these sufferings and sacrifices.» The formula of the offering was not always exact, but the meaning was always the same.

So much suffering began to undermine my mother's health. She was no longer able to work, so she sent for my sister Gloria to come and take care of her, and look after the house as well. All the surgeons and doctors around were consulted. We had recourse to every kind of remedy, but there was no improvement whatsoever. The good parish priest kindly offered to take my mother to Leiria in his mule cart, to consult the doctors there. Accompanied by my sister Teresa, she went to Leiria. But she arrived home half dead from such a journey, worn out after so many consultations, and having obtained no beneficial results of any kind. Finally, a surgeon in S. Mamede was consulted. He declared that my mother had a cardiac lesion, a dislocated spinal vertebra, and fallen kidneys. He prescribed for her a rigorous treatment of red-hot needles and various kinds of medication, and this brought about some improvement in her condition.

This is how things were with us when the 13th of May, 1917, arrived. It was around this time also that my brother reached the age for enlistment in the army. As his health was excellent, there was every reason to expect that he would be accepted. Besides, there was a war on, and it would be difficult to obtain his exemption from military service. My mother, afraid of being left alone and with no one to look after the land, sent also for my sister Carolina to come home. Meanwhile, my brother's godfather promised to obtain his exemption. He put in a word with the doctor responsible for his medical examination, and thus the good Lord deigned to grant my mother this relief.

Apparitions of Our Lady

I will not delay now describing the Apparition of May 13th. It is well known to Your Excellency, and it would therefore be waste of time for me to go into it here. You also know how my mother came to be aware of what happened, and how she spared no efforts to make me admit that I had lied. We agreed never to reveal to anyone the words that Our Lady spoke to us that day. After having promised to take us to heaven, she asked:

«Are you willing to offer yourselves to God to bear all the sufferings He wills to send you, as an act of reparation for the sins by which He is offended, and of supplication for the conversion of sinners?»

«Yes, we are willing,» was our reply.

«Then, you are going to have much to suffer, but the grace of God will be your comfort.»

The 13th of June, feast of St. Anthony, was always a day of great festivities in our parish. On that day, we usually let out the flocks very early in the morning, and at nine o'clock we shut them up in their pens again, and went off to the festa. My mother and my sisters, who knew how much I loved a festa, kept saying to me: «We've yet to see

67

if you'll leave the festa just to go to the Cova da Iria, and talk to that Lady!» On the day itself nobody said a single word to me. Insofar as I was concerned, they acted as if they were saying: «Leave her alone; and we'll soon see what she'll do!»

I let out my flock at daybreak, intending to put them back in the pen at nine, go to Mass at ten, and after that, go to the Cova da Iria. But the sun was no sooner up than my brother came to call me. He told me to go back home, as there were several people there wanting to speak to me. He himself stayed with the flock, and I went to see what they wanted. I found some women, and men too, who had come from such places as Minde, from around Tomar, Carrascos, Boleiros, etc. [21] They wished to accompany me to the Cova da Iria. I told them that it was early as yet, and invited them to go with me to the 8 o'clock Mass. After that, I returned home. These good people waited for me out in the yard, in the shade of our fig trees.

My mother and my sisters persisted in their contemptuous attitude, and this cut me to the heart, and was indeed as hurtful to me as insults.

Around 11 o'clock, I left home and called at my uncle's house, where Jacinta and Francisco were waiting for me. Then we set off for the Cova da Iria, in expectation of the longed-for moment. All those people followed us, asking a thousand questions. On that day, I was overwhelmed with bitterness. I could see that my mother was deeply distressed, and that she wanted at all costs to compel me, as she put it, to admit that I had lied. I wanted so much to do as she wished, but the only way I could do so was to tell a lie. From the cradle, she had instilled into her children a great horror of lying, and she used to chastise severely any one of us who told an untruth.

«I've seen to it,» she often said, «that my children always told the truth, and am I now to let the youngest get away with a thing like this? If it were just a small thing...! But a lie of such proportions, deceiving so many people and bringing them all the way here!» After these bitter complaints, she would turn to me, saying: «Make up your mind which you want! Either undo all this deception by telling these people that you've lied, or I'll lock you up in a dark room where you won't even see the light of the sun. After all the troubles I've been through, and now a thing like this to happen!» My

sisters sided with my mother, and all around me the atmos-
phere was one of utter scorn and contempt.

Then I would remember the old days, and ask myself:
«Where is all that affection now, that my family had for me
just such a short while ago?» My one relief was to weep
before the Lord, as I offered Him my sacrifice. It was on
this very day that, in addition to what I have already narrated,
Our Lady, as though guessing what was going on, said to me:

«Are you suffering a great deal? Don't lose heart. I will
never forsake you. My Immaculate Heart will be your refuge
and the way that will lead you to God.»

When Jacinta saw me in tears, she tried to console me,
saying:

«Don't cry. Surely, these are the sacrifices which the
Angel said that God was going to send us. That's why you
are suffering, so that you can make reparation to Him and
convert sinners.»

Lucia's Doubts and Temptations [22]

Around that time, our parish priest came to know of
what was happening, and sent word to my mother to take
me to his house. My mother felt she could breathe again,
thinking the priest was going to take responsibility for these
events on himself. She therefore said to me:

«Tomorrow, we're going to Mass, the first thing in the
morning. Then, you are going to the Reverend Father's house.
Just let him compel you to tell the truth, no matter how he
does it; let him punish you; let him do whatever he likes
with you, just so long as he forces you to admit that you
have lied; and then I'll be satisfied.»

My sisters also took my mother's part and invented end-
less threats, just to frighten me about the interview with the
parish priest. I told Jacinta and her brother all about it.

«We're going also,» they replied. «The Reverend Father
told our mother to take us there too, but she didn't say any
of those things to us. Never mind! If they beat us, we'll
suffer for love of Our Lord and for sinners.»

Next day [23] I walked along behind my mother, who did
not address one single word to me the whole way. I must
admit that I was trembling at the thought of what was going
to happen. During Mass, I offered my suffering to God.
Afterwards, I followed my mother out of the church over

to the priest's house, and started up the stairs leading to the verandah. We had climbed only a few steps, when my mother turned round and exclaimed:

«Don't annoy me any more! Tell the Reverend Father now that you lied, so that on Sunday he can say in the church that it was all a lie, and that will be the end of the whole affair. A nice business, this is! All this crowd running to the Cova da Iria, just to pray in front of a holm oak bush!»

Without more ado, she knocked on the door. The good priest's sister opened the door and invited us to sit down on a bench and wait a while.At last, the parish priest appeared. He took us into his study, motioned my mother to a seat, and beckoned me over to his desk. When I found that His Reverence was questioning me quite calmly, and with such a kindly manner, I was amazed. I was still fearful, however, of what was yet to come. The interrogation was very minute and, I would even venture to say, tiresome. His Reverence concluded with this brief observation:

«It doesn't seem to me like a revelation from heaven. It is usual in such cases for Our Lord to tell the souls to whom He makes such communications to give their confessor or parish priest an account of what has happened. But this child, on the contrary, keeps it to herself as far as she can. This may also be a deceit of the devil. We shall see. The future will show us what we are to think about it all.»

Encouragement from Jacinta and Francisco

How much this reflection made me suffer, only God knows, for He alone can penetrate our inmost heart. I began then to have doubts as to whether these manifestations might be from the devil, who was seeking by these means to make me lose my soul. As I heard people say that the devil always brings conflict and disorder, I began to think that, truly, ever since I had started seeing these things, our home was no longer the same, for joy and peace had fled. What anguish I felt! I made known my doubts to my cousins.

«No, it's not the devil!» replied Jacinta, «not at all! They say that the devil is very ugly and that he's down under the ground in hell! But that Lady is so beautiful, and we saw her go up to heaven!»

Our Lord made use of this to allay somewhat the doubts

I had. But during the course of that month, I lost all enthusiasm for making sacrifices and acts of mortification, and ended up hesitating as to whether it wouldn't be better to say that I had been lying, and so put an end to the whole thing.

«Don't do that!» exclaimed Jacinta and Francisco. «Don't you see that now you are going to tell a lie, and to tell lies is a sin?»

While in this state of mind, I had a dream which only increased the darkness of my spirit. I saw the devil laughing at having deceived me, as he tried to drag me down to hell. On finding myself in his clutches, I began to scream so loudly and call on Our Lady for help that I awakened my mother. She called out to me in alarm, and asked me what was the matter. I can't recall what I told her, but I do remember that I was so paralysed with fear that I couldn't sleep any more that night. This dream left my soul clouded over with real fear and anguish. My one relief was to go off by myself to some solitary place, there to weep to my heart's content. Even the company of my cousins began to seem burdensome, and for that reason, I began to hide from them as well. The poor children! At times, they would search for me, calling out my name and receiving no answer, but I was there all the while, hidden right close to them in some corner where they never thought of looking.

The 13th of July was close at hand, and I was still doubtful as to whether I should go. I thought to myself: «If it's the devil, why should I go to see him? If they ask me why I'm not going, I'll say that I'm afraid it might be the devil who is appearing to us, and for that reason I'm not going. Let Jacinta and Francisco do as they like; I'm not going back to the Cova da Iria any more.» My decision made, I was firmly resolved to act on it.

By the evening of the 12th, the people were already gathering, in anticipation of the events of the following day. I therefore called Jacinta and Francisco, and told them of my resolution.

«We're going,» they answered. «The Lady said we were to go.»

Jacinta volunteered to speak to the Lady, but she was so upset over my not going, that she started to cry. I asked the reason for her tears.

«Because you don't want to go!»

«No, I'm not going. Listen! If the Lady asks for me,

tell her I'm not going, because I'm afraid it may be the devil.»

I left them then, to go and hide, and so avoid having to speak to all the people who came looking for me to ask questions. My mother thought I was playing with the children of the village, when all the time I was hidden behind the bramble bushes in a neighbour's property which adjoined the Arneiro, a little to the east of the well which I have mentioned so many times already. She scolded me, as soon as I got home that night:

«A fine little plaster saint you are, to be sure! All the time you have left from minding the sheep, you do nothing but play, and what's more you have to do it in such a way that nobody can find you!»

On the following day, when it was nearly time to leave, I suddenly felt I had to go, impelled by a strange force that I could hardly resist. Then I set out, and called at my uncle's house to see if Jacinta was still there. I found her in her room, together with her brother Francisco, kneeling beside the bed, crying.

«Aren't you going then?» I asked.

«Not without you! We don't dare. Do come!»

«Yes, I'm going,» I replied.

Their faces lighted up with joy, and they set out with me.

Crowds of people were waiting for us along the road, and only with difficulty did we finally get there. This was the day on which Our Lady deigned to reveal to us the Secret. After that, to revive my flagging fervour, she said to us:

«Sacrifice yourselves for sinners, and say many times to Jesus, especially whenever you make some sacrifice: O Jesus, it is for love of You, for the conversion of sinners, and in reparation for the sins committed against the Immaculate Heart of Mary.»

Lucia's Mother has her Doubts

Thanks to our good Lord, this apparition dispelled the clouds from my soul and my peace was restored. My poor mother worried more and more, as she saw the crowds who came flocking from all parts.

«These poor people,» she said, «come here, taken in by your trickery, you can be sure of that, and I really don't know what I can do to undeceive them.»

A poor man who boasted of making fun of us, of insulting us and of even going so far as to beat us, asked my mother one day:

«Well, ma'am, what have you got to say about your daughter's visions?»

«I don't know,» she answered. «It seems to me that she's nothing but a fake, who is leading half the world astray.»

«Don't say that out loud, or somebody's likely to kill her. I think there are people around here, who'd be only too glad to do so.»

«Oh, I don't care, just so long as they force her to confess the truth. As for me, I always tell the truth, whether against my children, or anybody else, or even against myself.»

And, truly, this was so. My mother always told the truth, even against herself. We, her children, are indebted to her for this good example.

One day, she resolved to make a fresh attempt to compel me to retract all that I had said, as she put it. She made up her mind to take me back the very next day to the parish priest's house. Once there, I was to confess that I had lied, to ask his pardon, and to perform whatever penance His Reverence thought fit or desired to impose on me. This time the attack was so strong, that I did not know what to do. On the way, as I passed my uncle's house, I ran inside to tell Jacinta, who was still in bed, what was taking place. Then I hurried out and followed my mother. In my account about Jacinta, I have already told Your Excellency about the part played by her and her brother in this trial which the Lord had sent us, and how they prayed as they waited for me at the well, and so on.

As we walked along, my mother preached me a fine sermon. At a certain point, I said to her, trembling: «But, mother, how can I say that I did not see, when I did see?» My mother was silent. As we drew near the priest's house, she declared: «Just you listen to me! What I want is that you should tell the truth. If you saw, say so! But if you didn't see, admit that you lied.»

Without another word, we climbed the stairs, and the good priest received us in his study with the greatest kindness and even, I might almost say, with affection. He questioned me seriously, but most courteously, and resorted to various stratagems to see if I would contradict myself, or be inconsistent in my statements. Finally, he dismissed us, shrugging his shoulders, as if to imply: «I don't know what to make of all this!»

The Administrator's Threats

Not many days later, our parents were notified to the effect that all three of us, Jacinta, Francisco and myself, together with our fathers, were to appear at a given hour on the following day before the Administration in Vila Nova de Ourém. This meant that we had to make a journey of about nine miles, a considerable distance for three small children. The only means of transport in those days was either our own two feet or to ride on a donkey. My uncle sent word right away to say that he would appear himself, but as for his children, he was not taking them.

«They'd never stand the trip on foot,» he said, «and not being used to riding, they could never manage to stay on the donkey. And any way, there's no sense in bringing two children like that before a court.»

My parents thought the very opposite.

«My daughter is going. Let her answer for herself. As for me, I understand nothing of these things. If she's lying, it's a good thing that she should be punished for it.»

Very early next morning, they put me on a donkey and off I went, accompanied by my father and uncle. I fell off the donkey three times along the way. I think I have already told Your Excellency how much Jacinta and Francisco suffered that day, thinking that I was going to be killed. As for me, what hurt me most, was the indifference shown me by my parents. This was all the more obvious, since I could see how affectionately my aunt and uncle treated their children. I remember thinking to myself as we went along:

«How different my parents are from my uncle and aunt. They risk themselves to defend their children, while my parents hand me over with the greatest indifference, and let them do what they like with me! But I must be patient,» I reminded myself in my inmost heart, «since this means I have the happiness of suffering more for love of You, O my God, and for the conversion of sinners.» This reflection never failed to bring me consolation.

At the Administration office, I was interrogated by the Administrator, in the presence of my father, my uncle and several other gentlemen who were strangers to me. The Administrator was determined to force me to reveal the secret and to promise him never again to return to the Cova da Iria. To attain his end, he spared neither promises, nor even threats. Seeing that he was getting nowhere, he dismissed me, protesting however, that he would achieve his end, even if this meant that he had to take my life. He then strongly reprimanded my uncle for not having carried out his orders, and finally let us go home.

Trouble in Lucia's Family

In the intimacy of my own family, there was fresh trouble, and the blame for this was thrown on me. The Cova da Iria was a piece of land belonging to my parents. In the hollow, it was more fertile, and there we cultivated maize, greens, peas and other vegetables. On the slopes grew olive trees, oaks and holm oaks. Now, ever since the people began to go there, we had been unable to cultivate anything at all. Everything was trampled on. As the majority came mounted, their animals ate up all they could find and wrecked the whole place. My mother bewailed her loss: «You, now,» she said to me, «when you want something to eat, go and ask the Lady for it!» My sisters chimed in with: «Yes, you can have what grows in the Cova da Iria!»

These remarks cut me to the heart, so much so that I hardly dared to take a piece of bread to eat. To force me to tell the truth, as she said, my mother, more often than not, beat me soundly with the broom-handle or a stick from the woodpile near the fireplace. But in spite of this, mother that she was, she then tried to revive my failing strength. She was full of concern when she saw me so thin and pale, and feared I might fall sick. Poor mother! Now, indeed, that I understand what her situation really was, how sorry I feel for her! Truly, she was right to judge me unworthy of such a favour, and therefore to think I was lying.

By a special grace from Our Lord, I never experienced the slightest thought or feeling of resentment regarding her manner of acting towards me. As the Angel had announced that God would send me sufferings, I always saw the hand of God in it all. The love, esteem and respect which I owed her, went on increasing, just as though I were most dearly cherished. And now, I am more grateful to her for having treated me like this, than if she had continued to surround me with endearments and caresses.

Lucia's First Spiritual Director

It seems to me that it was in the course of this month [24] that Rev. Dr. Formigão came for the first time to question me. His interrogation was serious and detailed. I liked him very much, for he spoke to me a great deal about the practice of virtue, and taught me various ways of exercising myself in it. He showed me a holy picture of St. Agnes, told me about her martyrdom and encouraged me to imitate her. His Reverence continued to come every month for an interrogation, and always ended up by giving me some good advice, which was of help to me spiritually. One day he said to me:

«My child, you must love Our Lord very much, in return for so many favours and graces that He is granting you.»

These words made such an impression on my soul that, from then on, I acquired the habit of constantly saying to Our Lord: «My God, I love You, in thanksgiving for the graces which You have granted me.» I so loved this ejaculation, that I passed it on to Jacinta and her brother, who took it so much to heart that, in the middle of the most exciting games, Jacinta would ask: «Have you been forgetting to tell Our Lord how much you love Him for the graces He has given us?»

Imprisonment at Ourém

Meanwhile the 13th day of August had dawned. Ever since the previous evening, crowds had been pouring in from all parts. They all wanted to see and question us, and recommend their petitions to us, so that we could transmit them to the most Holy Virgin. In the middle of all that crowd, we were like a ball in the hands of boys at play. We were pulled hither and thither, everyone asking us questions without giving us a chance to answer anybody. In the midst of all this commotion, an order came from the Administrator, telling me to go to my aunt's house, where he was awaiting me. My father got the notification and it was he who took me there. When I arrived, he was in a room with my cousins. He interrogated us there, and made fresh attempts to force us to reveal the secret and to promise that we would not go back to the Cova da Iria. As he achieved nothing, he gave orders to my father and my uncle to take us to the parish priest's house.

I will not delay now to tell Your Excellency about every-thing else that happened during our imprisonment, for you already know it all. As I have previously explained to Your Excellency, what I felt most deeply and what caused me most suffering on that occasion was my being completely abandoned by my family; and it was the same for my little cousins. After this journey or imprisonment, for I really don't know what to call it, I returned home, as far as I can remem-ber, on the 15th of August. To celebrate my arrival, they sent me right away to let out the sheep and take them off to pasture. My uncle and aunt wanted their children to stay with them at home, and therefore sent their brother John in their place. As it was already late, we stayed in the vicinity of our little hamlet, at a place called Valinhos. [25]

What happened next, is also known to Your Excellency; therefore I will not delay here to describe this either. Once again, the most Blessed Virgin recommended to us the practice of mortification, and ended by saying:

«Pray, pray very much, and make sacrifices for sinners; for many souls go to hell, because there are none to sacrifice themselves and to pray for them.»

Penances and Sufferings

Some days later, as we were walking along the road with our sheep, I found a piece of rope that had fallen off a cart. I picked it up and, just for fun, I tied it round my arm. Before long, I noticed that the rope was hurting me.

«Look, this hurts!» I said to my cousins. «We could tie it round our waists and offer this sacrifice to God.»

The poor children promptly fell in with my suggestion. We then set about dividing it between the three of us, by placing it across a stone and striking it with the sharp edge of another one that served as a knife. Either because of the thickness or roughness of the rope, or because we sometimes tied it too tightly, this instrument of penance often caused us terrible suffering. Now and then, Jacinta could not keep back her tears, so great was the discomfort this caused her. Whenever I urged her to remove it, she replied: «No! I want to offer this sacrifice to Our Lord in reparation, and for the conversion of sinners.»

Another day we were playing, picking little plants off the walls and pressing them in our hands to hear them crack.

While Jacinta was plucking these plants, she happened to catch hold of some nettles and stung herself. She no sooner felt the pain than she squeezed them more tightly in her hands, and said to us: «Look! Look! Here is something else with which we can mortify ourselves!» From that time on, we used to hit our legs occasionally with nettles, so as to offer to God yet another sacrifice.

If I am not mistaken, it was also during this month that we acquired the habit of giving our lunch to our little poor children, as I have already described to Your Excellency in the account about Jacinta. It was during this month too, that my mother began to feel a little more at peace. She would say: «If there were even just one more person who had seen something, why then, I might believe! But among all those people, they're the only ones who saw anything!»

Now, during this past month, various people were saying that they had seen different things. Some had seen Our Lady, others, various signs in the sun, and so on. My mother declared: «I used to think before, that if there were just one other person who saw anything, then I'd believe; but now, so many people say they have seen something, and I still don't believe!» My father also began, about then, to come to my defence, and to silence those who started scolding me; as he used to say: «We don't know if it's true, but neither do we know if it's a lie.»

Then it was that my uncle and aunt, wearied by the troublesome demands of all these outsiders who were continually wanting to see us and speak to us, began to send their son John out to pasture the flock, and they themselves remained at home with Jacinta and Francisco. Shortly afterwards, they ended by selling the sheep altogether. As I did not enjoy any other company, I started to go out alone with my sheep. As I've already told Your Excellency, whenever I happened to be nearby, Jacinta and her brother would come to join me; and when the pasture was at a distance they would be waiting for me on my way home. I can truly say that these were really happy days. Alone, in the midst of my sheep, whether on the tops of the hills or in the depths of the valleys below, I contemplated the beauty of the heavens and thanked the good God for all the graces He had bestowed on me. When the voice of one of my sisters broke in on my solitude, calling for me to go back home to talk to some person or other who had come looking for me, I felt a keen displeasure, and my only consolation was to be able to offer up to our dear Lord yet another sacrifice.

On a certain day, three gentlemen came to speak to us. After their questioning, which was anything but pleasant, they took their leave with this remark: «See that you decide to tell that secret of yours. If you don't, the Administrator has every intention of taking your lives!» Jacinta, her face lighting up with a joy that she made no effort to hide, said: «How wonderful! I so love Our Lord and Our Lady, and this way we'll be seeing them soon!» The rumour got round that the Administrator did really intend to kill us. This led my aunt, who was married and lived in Casais, to come to our house with the express purpose of taking us home with her, for, as she explained: «I live in another district and, therefore, this Administrator cannot lay hands on you there.» But her plan was never carried out, because we were unwilling to go, and replied: «If they kill us, it's all the same! We'll go to heaven!»

September 13th

Now the 13th of September was drawing near. In addition to what I have already related, Our Lady said to us on this day:

«God is pleased with your sacrifices, but He does not want you to sleep with the rope on; only wear it during the day.»

Needless to say, we promptly obeyed His orders. Since it seems Our Lord had, a month before, wished to give some visible sign out of the ordinary, my mother eagerly hoped that, on this day, such signs would be still more clear and evident. The good Lord, however, perhaps to give us the opportunity to offer Him yet another sacrifice, permitted that no ray of His glory should appear on this day. My mother lost heart once more, and the persecution at home began all over again. She had indeed many reasons for being so upset. The Cova da Iria was now a total loss, not only as a fine pasture for our flock, but even as regards the eatables we had grown there. Added to this was my mother's almost certain conviction, as she expressed it, that the events themselves were nothing but foolish fancies and mere childish imaginings. One of my sisters did scarcely anything else but go and call me, and take my place with the flock, while I went to speak to the people who were asking to see me and talk to me.

This waste of time would have meant nothing to a wealthy family, but for ourselves, who had to live by our work, it meant a great deal. After some time, my mother found herself obliged to sell our flock, and this made no small difference to the support of the family. I was blamed for the whole thing, and at critical moments, it was all flung in my face. I hope our dear Lord has accepted it all from me, for I offered it to Him, always happy to be able to sacrifice myself for Him and for sinners. On her part, my mother endured everything with heroic patience and resignation; and if she reprimanded me and punished me, it was because she really thought that I was lying. She was completely resigned to the crosses which Our Lord was sending her, and at times she would say: «Could it be that all this is God's work, in punishment for my sins? If so, then blessed be God!»

Lucia's Spirit of Sacrifice

A neighbour took it upon herself one day, why I don't know, to remark that some gentlemen had given me some money, though I cannot remember how much. Without more ado, my mother called me and asked for it. When I told her I hadn't received any, she wanted to force me to hand it over to her, and to this end, had recourse to the broom-handle. When the dust had been well beaten out of my clothes, Carolina, one of my sisters, intervened, along with a girl from our neighbourhood called Virginia. They said they had been present at the interrogation, and they had seen that the gentlemen had actually given me nothing at all. Thanks to their defending me, I was able to slip away to my beloved well, and there offer yet another sacrifice to our good Lord.

A Tall Visitor

If I am not mistaken, it was also during this month [26] that a young man made his appearance at our home. He was of such tall stature that I trembled with fear. When I saw that he had to bend down in order to come through the doorway in search of me, I thought I must be in the presence of a German. At that time we were at war, and grown-ups would try to frighten children by saying: «Here comes a German to kill you.»

I thought, therefore, that my last hour had come. My fright did not pass unnoticed by the young man, who sought to calm me; he made me sit on his knee and questioned me with great kindness. His interrogation over, he asked my mother to let me go and show him the site of the apparitions, and pray with him there. He obtained the desired permission and off we went. But, all along the way, I trembled with fear at finding myself alone in the company of this stranger. Then I began to feel tranquil again at the thought that if he killed me, I would go to see Our Lord and Our Lady.

On arriving at the place, he knelt down and asked me to pray the Rosary with him to obtain a special grace from Our Lady that he greatly desired: that a certain young lady would consent to receive with him the sacrament of matrimony. I wondered at such a request, and thought to myself: «If she has as much fear of him as I, she will never say Yes!» When the Rosary was over, the good young man accompanied me most of the way home, and then bade me a friendly farewell, recommending his request to me again. I ran off helter skelter to my aunt's house, still afraid he might turn round and come back!

What was my surprise then, on the 13th of October, when I suddenly found myself, after the apparitions, in the arms of this same person, sailing along over the heads of the people. It actually served to satisfy the curiosity of everybody who wanted to see me! After a little while, the good man, who was unable to see where he was going, stumbled and fell. I didn't fall, as I was caught in the crush of people who pressed around me. Right away, others took hold of me, and this gentleman disappeared. It was not until some time later that he appeared again, this time accompanied by the aforesaid girl, who was now his wife! He came to thank the Blessed Virgin for the grace received, and to ask her copious blessings on their future. This young man is today Dr. Carlos Mendes of Torres Novas.

October 13th

Now, Your Excellency, here we are at the 13th of October. You already know all that happened on that day. Of all the words spoken at this Apparition, the ones most deeply engraved upon my heart were those of the request made by our heavenly Mother:

«Do not offend Our Lord and God any more, because He is already so much offended!» How loving a complaint, how tender a request! Who will grant me to make it echo through the whole world, so that all the children of our Mother in heaven may hear the sound of her voice!

The rumour had spread that the authorities intended to explode a bomb quite close to us, at the very moment of the Apparition. This did not frighten me in the least. I spoke of it to my cousins. «How wonderful!» we exclaimed, «if we were granted the grace of going up to heaven from there, together with Our Lady!» My parents, however, were very much afraid, and for the first time they wished to accompany me, saying that if their daughter was going to die, they wanted to die by her side. My father then took me by the hand to the place of the Apparitions. But from the moment of the Apparition itself, I did not set eyes on him again until I was back home with the family that night.

I spent the afternoon of that day with my cousins. We were like some curious creature that the multitudes wanted to see and observe. By night time I was really exhausted after so many questions and interrogations. These did not even end with nightfall. Several people, who had been unable to question me, remained over till the following day, awaiting their turn. Some of them even tried to talk to me that night, but, overcome by weariness, I just dropped down and fell asleep on the floor. Thank God, human respect and self-love were, at that time, still unknown to me. For that reason, I was as much at ease with any person at all, as I was with my parents.

On the following day, or rather, to be accurate, on the following days, the questionings continued. Almost every day, from then on, people went to the Cova da Iria to implore the protection of our heavenly Mother. Everybody wanted to see the seers, to put questions to them, and to recite the Rosary with them. At times, I was so tired of saying the same thing over and over again, and also of praying, that I looked for any pretext for excusing myself, and making my escape. But those poor people were so insistent, that I had to make an effort, and indeed no small effort, in order to satisfy them. I then repeated my usual prayer deep down in my heart: «O my God, it is for love of You, in reparation for the sins committed against the Immaculate Heart of Mary, for the conversion of sinners, and for the Holy Father!»

Questioned by Priests

In the account I have written about my cousin, I have already told Your Excellency how two holy priests came and spoke to us about His Holiness, and told us of his great need of prayers. From that time on, there was not a prayer or sacrifice that we offered to God which did not include an invocation for His Holiness. We grew to love the Holy Father so deeply, that when the parish priest told my mother that I would probably have to go to Rome to be interrogated by His Holiness, I clapped my hands with joy and said to my cousins: «Won't it be wonderful if I can go and see the Holy Father!» They burst into tears and said: «We can't go, but we can offer this sacrifice for him.»

The parish priest questioned me for the last time. [27] The events had duly come to an end at the appointed time, and still His Reverence did not know what to say about the whole affair. He was also beginning to show his displeasure. «Why are all those people going to prostrate themselves in prayer in a deserted spot like that, while here the Living God of our altars, in the Blessed Sacrament, is left all alone, abandoned, in the tabernacle? What's all that money for, the money they leave for no purpose whatsoever under that holmoak, while the church, which is under repairs, cannot be completed for lack of funds?» [28]

I understood perfectly why he spoke like that, but what could I do! If I had been given authority over the hearts of those people, I would certainly have led them to the parish church, but as I had not, I offered to God yet another sacrifice.

As Jacinta was in the habit of putting her head down, keeping her eyes fixed on the ground and scarcely uttering a word during the interrogations, I was usually called upon to satisfy the curiosity of the pilgrims. For that reason, I was continually being summoned to the house of the parish priest. On one occasion, a priest from Torres Novas came to question me. [29] When he did so, he went into such minute details, and tried so hard to trip me up, that afterwards I felt some scruples about having concealed certain things from him. I consulted my cousins on the matter:

«I don't know,» I asked them, «if we are doing wrong

by not telling everything, when they ask us if Our Lady told us anything else. When we just say that she told us a secret, I don't know whether we are lying or not, by saying nothing about the rest.»

«I don't know,» replied Jacinta, «that's up to you! You're the one who does not want us to say anything.»

«Of course I don't want you to say anything,» I answered. «Why, they'll start asking us what sort of mortifications we are practising! And that would be the last straw! Listen! If you had kept quiet, and not said a word, nobody would have known by now that we saw Our Lady, or spoke to her, or to the Angel; and nobody needed to know it anyway!»

The poor child had no sooner heard my arguments than she started to cry. Just as she did in May, she asked my forgiveness in the way I have already described in my account of her life. So I was left with my scruple, and had no idea as to how I was to resolve my doubt.

A little while later, another priest appeared; he was from Santarém. He looked like a brother of the first I've just spoken of, or at least they seemed to have rehearsed things together: asking the same questions, making the same attempts to trip me up, laughing and making fun of me in the same way; in fact their very height and features were almost identical. After this interrogation, my doubt was stronger than ever, and I really did not know what course of action to follow. I constantly pleaded with Our Lord and Our Lady to tell me what to do. «O my God, and my dearest Mother in heaven, you know that I do not want to offend you by telling lies; but you are well aware that it would not be right to tell them all that you told me!»

In the midst of this perplexity, I had the happiness of speaking to the Vicar of Olival. [30] I do not know why, but His Reverence inspired me with confidence, and I confided my doubt to him. I have already explained, in my account of Jacinta, how he taught us to keep our secret. He also gave us some further instructions on the spiritual life. Above all, he taught us to give pleasure to Our Lord in everything, and how to offer Him countless little sacrifices. «If you feel like eating something, my children,» he would say, «leave it, and eat something else instead; and thus offer a sacrifice to God. If you feel inclined to play, do not do so, and offer to God another sacrifice. If people question you, and you cannot avoid answering them, it is God who wills it so: offer Him this sacrifice too.»

This holy priest spoke a language that I could really understand, and I loved him dearly. From then on, he never lost sight of my soul. Now and then, he called in to see me, or kept in touch with me through a pious widow called Senhora Emilia [31] who lived in a little hamlet near Olival. She was very devout, and often went to pray at the Cova da Iria. After that, she used to come to our house and ask them to let me go and spend a few days with her. Then we paid a visit to the Reverend Vicar, who was kind enough to invite me to remain for two or three days as company for one of his sisters. At such times, he was patient enough to spend whole hours alone with me, teaching me the practice of virtue and guiding me with his own wise counsels. Even though at that time I did not understand anything about spiritual direction, I can truly say that he was my first spiritual director. I cherish, therefore, grateful and holy memories of this saintly priest.

111. AFTER THE APPARITIONS

Lucia Goes to School

Oh dear, here I am writing without rhyme or reason, as we say, and already leaving out various things that I should have said! But I am doing as Your Excellency told me: writing just what I remember and in all simplicity. That is what I want to do, without worrying about order or style. In that way, I think my obedience is more perfect, and therefore, more pleasing to Our Lord and to the Immaculate Heart of Mary.

I will go back, then, to my parents' home. I have told Your Excellency that my mother had to sell our flock. We kept only three sheep, which we took along with us when we went to the fields. Whenever we stayed at home, we kept them in the pen and fed them there. My mother then sent me to school, and in my free time, she wanted me to learn weaving and sewing. In this way, she had me safe in the house, and didn't have to waste any time looking for me. One fine day, my sisters were asked to go with some other girls to help with the vintage on the property of a wealthy man of Pé de Cão. [32] My mother decided to let them go, as long as I could go too. I have already said earlier on, that my mother never allowed them to go anywhere, unless they took me with them.

Lucia and the Parish Priest

At that time also, the parish priest began preparing the children for a solemn Communion. Since the age of six, I had repeated my solemn Communion every year, but this year my mother decided I would not do so. For this reason, I did not attend the Catechism classes. After school, the other children went to the parish priest's verandah, while I went home to get on with my sewing or weaving. The good priest did not take kindly to my absence from the Catechism classes. One day, on my way home from school, his sister sent another child after me. She caught up with me on the road to Aljustrel, near the house of a poor man who was nicknamed «Snail». She told me that the parish priest's sister wanted me, and that I was to go straight back.

Thinking that I was just wanted for questioning, I excused myself, saying that my mother had told me to go home right after school. Without further ado, I took to my heels across the fields like a mad thing, in search of a hiding place where no one could find me. But this time, the prank cost me dear. Some days later, there was a big feast in the parish, and several priests came from all around to sing the Mass. When it was over, the parish priest sent for me, and in front of all those priests, reprimanded me severely for not attending the catechism lessons, and for not running back to his sister when she had sent for me. In short, all my faults and failings were brought to light, and the sermon went on for quite a long while.

At last, though I don't know how, a holy priest appeared on the scene, and sought to plead my cause. He tried to excuse me, saying that perhaps my mother had not given me permission. But the good priest replied: «Her mother! Why, she's a saint! But as for this one, it remains to be seen what she'll turn out to be!»

The good priest, who later became Vicar of Torres Novas, then asked me very kindly why I had not been to the catechism classes. I therefore told him of my mother's decision. His Reverence did not seem to believe me, and sent for my sister Gloria who was over by the church, to find out the truth of the matter. Having found that indeed things were just as I had said, he came to this conclusion: «Well then! Either the child is going to attend the catechism classes for the days still remaining, and afterwards come to me for confession, and then make her solemn Communion with all the rest of the children, or she's never going to receive Communion again in this parish!»

When my sister heard this proposal, she pointed out that I was due to leave with my sisters five days beforehand, and such an arrangement would be most inconvenient. She added that, if His Reverence so desired, I could go to Confession and Communion some other day before we left. The good priest paid no attention to her request, and stood firm by his decision.

When we reached home, we told my mother all about it. She also went to the Reverend Father to ask him to hear my confession and give me Holy Communion on another day. But it was all in vain. My mother then decided that, after the solemn Communion day, my brother would make the journey with me, in spite of the long distance and the difficulties caused by the extremely bad roads, winding up and down the hills and highlands. I think I must have sweated ink at the mere idea of having to go to confession to the parish priest! I was so upset that I cried.

On the day before the solemn Communion, His Reverence sent for all the children to go to church in the afternoon to make their confession. As I went, anguish gripped my heart as in a vice. As I entered the church, I saw that there were several priests hearing confessions. There at the end of the church was Reverend Father Cruz from Lisbon. I had spoken to His Reverence before, and I liked him very much indeed.

Without noticing that the parish priest was in an open confessional halfway up the church, I thought to myself: «First, I'll go and make my confession to Father Cruz and ask him what I am to do, and then I'll go to the parish priest.» Dr. Cruz received me with the greatest kindness. After hearing my confession, he gave me some advice, telling me that if I did not want to go to the parish priest, I should not do so; and that he could not refuse me Communion for something like that. I was radiant with joy on hearing this advice and said my penance. Then I made good my escape from the church, for fear lest somebody might call me back. Next day, I went to the church all dressed in white, still afraid that I might be refused Communion. But His Reverence contented himself with letting me know, when the feast was over, that my lack of obedience in going to confession to another priest had not passed unnoticed.

The good priest grew more and more displeased and perplexed concerning these events until, one day, he left the parish. The news then went round that His Reverence had left on account of me, [33] because he did not want to assume responsibility for these events. He was a zealous priest and much beloved among the people, and so I had much to suffer as a result. Several pious women, whenever they met me, gave vent to their displeasure by insulting me; and sometimes sent me on my way with a couple of blows or kicks.

Companions in Sympathy and in Sacrifice

These heaven-sent «caresses» were rarely meted out to Jacinta and Francisco, for their parents would not allow anyone to lay hands on them. But they suffered when they saw me suffering, and many a time tears ran down their cheeks whenever they saw me distressed or humiliated.

One day, Jacinta said to me: «If only my parents were like yours, so that those people would beat me too, then I'd have more sacrifices to offer Our Lord.» However, she knew how to make the most of opportunities for mortifying herself. Occasionally also, we were in the habit of offering to God the sacrifice of spending nine days or a month without taking a drink. Once, we made this sacrifice even in the month of August, when the heat was suffocating. As we were returning, one day, from the Cova da Iria where we had been praying our Rosary, we came to a pond beside the road, and Jacinta said to me:

«Oh, I'm so thirsty, and my head aches so! I'm going to drink a little drop of this water.»

«Not that water,» I answered. «My mother doesn't want us to drink it, because it's not good for us. We'll go and ask Maria dos Anjos for some.» (She was a neighbour of ours, who had recently married and was living near there in a small house).

«No! I don't want good water. I'd rather drink this, because instead of offering Our Lord our thirst, I could offer Him the sacrifice of drinking this dirty water.»

As a matter of fact, this water was filthy. People washed their clothes in it, and the animals came there to drink and waded right into it. That was why my mother warned her children not to drink this water.

At other times, Jacinta would say:

«Our Lord must be pleased with our sacrifices, because I am so thirsty, so thirsty! Yet I do not want to take a drink. I want to suffer for love of Him.»

One day, we were sitting in the doorway of my uncle's house, when we noticed several people approaching. Not having time to do anything else, Francisco and I ran inside to hide under the beds, he in one room and I in another. Jacinta said:

«I'm not going to hide. I'm going to offer this sacrifice to Our Lord.»

These people came up and talked to her, waiting around quite a long time until I could be found. Finally, they went away. I slipped out of my hiding-place and asked Jacinta:

«What did you answer when they asked if you knew where we were?»

«I said nothing at all. I put my head down, kept my eyes fixed on the ground, and said nothing. I always do that, when I don't want to tell the truth; and I don't want to tell a lie either, because lying is a sin.»

She was indeed accustomed to do just this, and it was useless to question her, for those who did so obtained no response whatsoever. If escape were at all possible, we normally felt little inclined to offer this kind of sacrifice.

Another day, we were sitting in the shade of two fig trees overhanging the road that runs by my cousins' house. Francisco began to play a little way off. He saw several ladies coming towards us and ran back to warn us. We promptly climbed up the fig trees. In those days it was the fashion to wear hats with brims as wide as a sieve, and we were sure that with such headgear, those people would never catch sight of us up there. As soon as the ladies had gone by, we came down as fast as we could, took to our heels and hid in a cornfield.

This habit we had of making good our escape, whenever possible, was yet another cause for complaint on the part of the parish priest. He bitterly complained of the way we tried to avoid priests in particular. His Reverence was certainly right. It was priests especially who put us through the most rigorous cross-examinations, and then returned to question us all over again. Whenever we found ourselves in the presence of a priest, we prepared to offer to God one of our greatest sacrifices!

Government Opposition

Meanwhile, the Government showed disapproval of the way affairs were progressing. At the place of the Apparitions some people had erected poles to form an arch, hung with lanterns which they were careful to keep always burning. One night orders were given for some men to pull down these poles, and also cut down the holmoak on which the Apparitions had taken place, and drag it away with them behind a car. In the morning, news of what had happened spread like wildfire. I ran to the place to see if it were true. But what was my delight to find that the poor men had made a mistake, and that instead of cutting down the holmoak, they had carried off one of the others growing nearby! I then asked Our Lady to forgive these poor men, and I prayed for their conversion.

Some time later, on the 13th of May, I don't remember whether it was in 1918 or 1919, [34] news went round at dawn that cavalrymen were in Fatima to prevent the people from going to the Cova da Iria. Everybody was alarmed, and came to give me the news, assuring me that without any doubt this was to be the last day of my life. Without taking this news too seriously, I set out for the church. When I reached Fatima, I passed between the horses which were all over the church grounds, and went into the church. I heard a Mass celebrated by a priest I did not know, received Holy Communion, made my thanksgiving, and went back home without anyone saying a single word to me. I don't know whether it was because they did not see me, or that they did not think me worthy of notice.

News kept coming in that the troops were trying in vain to keep people away from the Cova da Iria. In spite of this, I went there, too, to recite the Rosary. On the way I was joined by a group of women who had come from a distance. As we drew near the place, two cavalrymen gave their horses a smart crack of the whip and advanced at full speed towards the group. They pulled up beside us and asked where we were going. The women boldly replied that «it was none of their business». They whipped the horses again, as though they meant to charge forward and trample us all underfoot. The women ran in all directions and, a moment later, I found myself alone with the two cavalrymen. They then asked me my name, and I gave it without hesitation. They next asked if I were the seer, and I said I was. They ordered me to step out on to the middle of the road between the two horses, and proceed in the direction of Fatima.

As we reached the pond I spoke of earlier, a poor woman who lived there and whom I have also mentioned, seeing me coming in the distance between the two horses, ran out, as I approached, into the middle of the road, like another Veronica. The soldiers lost no time in getting her out of the way, and the poor woman burst into a flood of tears, loudly bewailing my misfortune. A few paces further on, they stopped and asked me if the woman was my mother. I said she was not. They did not believe me, and asked if that house was my home. I again said «No». Still apparently not believing me, they ordered me to walk a little ahead until I arrived at my parents' house.

When we reached a plot of ground that lies on the outskirts of Aljustrel, where there was a small spring, and some trenches dug for planting vines, they called a halt, and said to one another, probably in order to frighten me:

«Here are some open trenches. Let's cut off her head with one of our swords, and leave her here dead and buried. Then we'll be finished with this business once and for all.»

When I heard these words, I thought that my last moment had really come, but I was as much at peace as if it did not concern me at all. After a minute or two during which they seemed to be thinking it over, the other replied:

«No, we have no authority to do such a thing.»

They ordered me to keep on going. So I went straight through our little village, until I arrived at my parents' house. All the neighbours were at the windows and doors of their houses to see what was going on. Some were laughing and making fun of me, others lamenting my sorry plight. When we reached my home, they ordered me to call my parents, but they were not at home. One of them dismounted and went to see if my parents were hiding inside. He searched the house, but found no one; whereupon he gave orders for me to stay indoors for the rest of the day. Then he mounted his horse and they both rode off.

Late in the afternoon, news went round that the troops had withdrawn, defeated by the people. At sunset, I was praying my Rosary in the Cova da Iria, accompanied by hundreds of people. While I was under arrest, according to what we heard later, some persons went to tell my mother what was happening, and she replied: «If it's true that she saw Our Lady, Our Lady will defend her; and if she's lying, it will serve her right to be punished.» And she remained in peace as before. Now, some one will ask me: «And where were your little companions, while this was going on?» I don't know. I can recall nothing at all of their whereabouts at that time. Perhaps, in view of the news that got abroad, their parents did not allow them to leave the house at all that day.

Lucia's Mother Falls Seriously ill

Such suffering on my part must have been pleasing to Our Lord, because He was about to prepare a most bitter chalice for me which He was soon to give me to drink. My mother fell so seriously ill that, at one stage, we thought she was dying. All her children gathered around her bed to receive her last blessing, and to kiss the hand of their dying mother. As I was the youngest, my turn came last. When my poor mother saw me, she brightened a little, flung her arms around my neck and, with a deep sigh, exclaimed: «My poor daughter, what will become of you without your mother! I am dying with my heart pierced through because of you.» Then, bursting into tears and sobbing bitterly, she clasped me more and more tightly in her arms.

My eldest sister forcibly pulled me away from my mother, took me to the kitchen and forbade me to go back to the sick room, saying: «Mother is going to die of grief because of all the trouble you've given her!» I knelt down, put my head on a bench, and in a distress more bitter than any I had ever known before, I made the offering of my sacrifice to our dear Lord. A few minutes later, my two older sisters, thinking the case was hopeless, came to me and said: «Lucia! If it is true that you saw Our Lady, go right now to the Cova da Iria, and ask her to cure our mother. Promise her whatever you wish and we'll do it; and then we'll believe.»

Without losing a moment, I set out. So as not to be seen, I made my way across the fields along some bypaths, reciting the Rosary all the way. Once there, I placed my request before Our Lady and unburdened myself of all my sorrow, shedding copious tears. I then went home, comforted by the hope that my beloved Mother in heaven would hear my prayer and restore health to my mother on earth. When I reached home, my mother was already feeling somewhat better. Three days later, she was able to resume her work around the house.

I had promised the most Blessed Virgin that, if she granted me what I asked, I would go there for nine days in succession, together with my sisters, pray the Rosary and go on our knees from the roadway to the holmoak tree; and on the ninth day we would take nine poor children with us, and afterwards give them a meal. We went, then, to fulfil my promise, and my mother came with us.

«How strange!» she said. «Our Lady cured me, and somehow I still don't believe! I don't know how this can be!»

Lucia's Father Dies

Our good Lord gave me this consolation, but once again He came knocking on my door to ask yet another sacrifice, and not a small one either. My father was a healthy man, and robust; he said he had never known what it was to have a headache. But, in less than twenty-four hours, an attack of double pneumonia carried him off into eternity. [35] My sorrow was so great that I thought I would die as well. He was the only one who never failed to show himself to be my friend, and the only one who defended me when disputes arose at home on account of me.

«My God! My God!» I exclaimed in the privacy of my room. «I never thought You had so much suffering in store for me! But I suffer for love of You, in reparation for the sins committed against the Immaculate Heart of Mary, for the Holy Father and for the conversion of sinners.»

Serious Illness of Lucia's Cousins

Around that time, Jacinta and Francisco also began to grow worse. [36] Jacinta used to tell me sometimes:

«My chest hurts so much, but I'm not saying anything to my mother! I want to suffer for Our Lord, in reparation for the sins committed against the Immaculate Heart of Mary, for the Holy Father and for the conversion of sinners.» One morning, when I went to see her, she asked me:

«How many sacrifices did you offer to Our Lord last night?»

«Three. I got up three times to recite the Angel's prayers.»

«Well, I offered Him many, many sacrifices. I don't know how many there were, but I had a lot of pain, and I made no complaint.»

Francisco spoke very little. He usually did everything he saw us doing, and rarely suggested anything himself. During his illness, he suffered with heroic patience, without ever letting the slightest moan or the least complaint escape his lips. One day, shortly before his death, I asked him:

«Are you suffering a lot, Francisco?»

«Yes, but I suffer it all for love of Our Lord and Our Lady.»

One day, he gave me the rope that I have already spoken about, saying:

«Take it away before my mother sees it. I don't feel able to wear it any more around my waist.»

He took everything his mother offered him, and she could never discover which things he disliked. He went on like this until the day came for him to go to heaven. [37] The day before his death, he said to Jacinta and myself:

«I am going to heaven, but when I'm there, I will pray a great deal to Our Lord and Our Lady, asking them to bring you there, too, very soon.»

I think I have already described, in my account of Jacinta, what suffering this separation caused us. For this reason, I do not repeat it here. Jacinta was already very sick, and was gradually growing worse. There is no need to describe it now, as I have already done so. I shall simply relate one or two acts of virtue, which I saw her practise, and which I do not think I have described before.

Her mother knew how hard it was for her to take milk. So, one day, she brought her a fine bunch of grapes with her cup of milk, saying:

«Jacinta, take this. If you can't take the milk, leave it there, and eat the grapes.»

«No, mother, I don't want the grapes; take them away, and give me the milk instead. I'll take that.» Then, without showing the least sign of repugnance, she took it. My aunt went happily away, thinking her little girl's appetite was returning. She had no sooner gone than Jacinta turned to me and said:

«I had such a longing for those grapes and it was so hard to drink the milk! But I wanted to offer this sacrifice to Our Lord.»

One morning, I found her looking dreadful, and I asked her if she felt worse.

«Last night,» she answered, «I had so much pain, and I wanted to offer Our Lord the sacrifice of not turning over in bed; therefore I didn't sleep at all.»

On another occasion, she told me:

«When I'm alone, I get out of bed to recite the angel's prayer. But now I'm not able to touch the ground any more with my head, because I fall over; so I only pray on my knees.»

One day, I had the opportunity of speaking to the Vicar. His Reverence asked me about Jacinta and how she was. I told him what I thought about her condition, and afterwards related what she had said to me about being unable to touch the ground when she prayed. His Reverence sent me to tell her that she was not to get out of bed in order to pray, but that she was to pray lying down, and then only as long as she could do so without getting tired. I delivered the message at the very first opportunity.

«And will Our Lord be pleased?» she asked.

«He is pleased,» I replied. «Our Lord wants us to do whatever the Reverend Vicar says.»

«That's alright, then. I won't get up any more.»

Whenever I could, I loved to go to the Cabeço to pray in our favourite cave. Jacinta was very fond of flowers, and coming down the hillside on the way home, I used to pick a bunch of irises and peonies, when there were any to be found, and take them to her, saying:

«Look! These are from the Cabeço!» She would take them

eagerly, and sometimes, with tears running down her cheeks, she would say:

«To think I'll never go there again! Nor to Valinhos, nor Cova da Iria! I miss them all so much!»

«But what does it matter, if you're going to heaven to see Our Lord and Our Lady?»

«That's true.» she replied.

Then she lay there contentedly, plucking off the petals and counting them one by one.

A few days after falling ill, she gave me the rope she had been wearing, and said:

«Keep it for me; I'm afraid my mother may see it. If I get better, I want it back again!»

This cord had three knots, and was somewhat stained with blood. I kept it hidden until I finally left my mother's home. Then, not knowing what to do with it, I burned it, and Francisco's as well.

Lucia in Poor Health

Several people who came from a distance to see us, noticing that I looked very pale and anaemic, asked my mother to let me go and spend a few days in their homes, saying the change of air would do me good. With this end in view, my mother gave her consent, and they took me with them, now to one place, now to another.

When away from home like this, I did not always meet with esteem and affection. While there were some who admired me and considered me a saint, there were always others who heaped abuse upon me and called me a hypocrite, a visionary and a sorceress. This was the good Lord's way of throwing salt into the water to prevent it from going bad. Thanks to this Divine Providence, I went through the fire without being burned, or without becoming acquainted with the little worm of vanity which has the habit of gnawing its way into everything. On such occasions, I used to think to myself: «They are all mistaken. I'm not a saint, as some say, and I'm not a liar either, as others say. Only God knows what I am.» When I got home, I would run to see Jacinta, who said:

«Listen! Don't go away again. I have been so lonely for you! Since you went away, I have not spoken to anyone. I don't know how to talk to other people.»

The time finally came for Jacinta to leave for Lisbon. I have already described our leave-taking, and therefore I won't repeat it here. How sad I was to find myself alone! In such a short space of time, our dear Lord had taken to heaven my beloved father, and then Francisco; and now He was taking Jacinta, whom I was never to see again in this world. As soon as I could, I slipped away to the Cabeço, and hid within our cave among the rocks. There, alone with God, I poured forth my grief and shed tears in abundance. Coming back down the slope, everything reminded me of my dear companions: the stones on which we had so often sat, the flowers I no longer picked, not having anyone to take them to; Valinhos, where the three of us had enjoyed the delights of paradise! As though I had lost all sense of reality, and still half abstracted, I went into my aunt's house one day and made for Jacinta's room, calling out to her. Her sister Teresa, seeing me like that, barred the way, and reminded me that Jacinta was no longer there!

Shortly afterwards, news arrived that she had taken flight to heaven. [38] Her body was then brought back to Vila Nova de Ourém. My aunt took me there one day to pray beside the mortal remains of her little daughter, in the hope of thus distracting me. But for a long time after, my sorrow seemed only to grow ever greater. Whenever I found the cemetery open, I went and sat by Francisco's grave, or beside my father's, and there I spent long hours.

My mother, thank God, decided some time after this to go to Lisbon, and to take me with her. [39] Through the kindness of Dr. Formigão, a good lady received us into her house, and offered to pay for my education in a boarding-school, if I was willing to remain. My mother and I gratefully accepted the generous offer of this charitable lady, whose name was Dona Assunção Avelar. My mother, after consulting the doctors, found that she needed an operation for kidneys and spinal column; but the doctors would not be responsible for her life, since she also suffered from a cardiac lesion. She therefore went home, leaving me in the care of this lady. When everything was ready, and the day arranged for my entering the boarding school, I was informed that the Government was aware that I was in Lisbon, and was seeking my whereabouts. They, therefore, took me to Santarém to Dr. Formigão's house, and for some days I remained hidden, without even being allowed out to Mass.

Finally, His Reverence's sister arrived to take me home to my mother, promising to arrange for my admittance to a boarding school that the Dorothean Sisters had in Spain, and assuring us that as soon as everything was settled, she would come and fetch me. All these happenings distracted me somewhat, and so the oppressive sadness began to disappear.

Lucia's First Meeting with the Bishop

It was about this time that Your Excellency was installed as Bishop of Leiria, and our dear Lord confided to your care this poor flock that had been for so many years without a shepherd. [40] There were not wanting people who tried to frighten me about Your Excellency's arrival, just as they had done before about another holy priest. They told me that Your Excellency knew everything, that you could read hearts and penetrate the depths of consciences, and that now you were going to discover all my deception. Far from frightening me, it made me earnestly desire to speak to you, and I thought to myself: «If it's true that he knows everything, he will know that I am speaking the truth.» For this reason, as soon as a kind lady from Leiria offered to take me to see Your Excellency, I accepted her suggestion with joy. There was I, full of hope, in expectation of this happy moment. At last the day came, and the lady and I went to the Palace. We were invited to enter, and shown to a room, where we were asked to wait for a little while.

A few moments later, Your Excellency's Secretary came in, [41] and spoke kindly with Dona Gilda who accompanied me. From time to time, he asked me some questions. As I had already been twice to confession to His Reverence, I already knew him, and it was therefore a pleasure to talk to him. A little later, Rev. Dr. Marques dos Santos [42] came in, wearing shoes with buckles, and wrapped in a great big cloak. As it was the first time that I had seen a priest dressed like this, it caught my attention.

He then embarked on a whole repertoire of questions that seemed unending. Now and again, he laughed, as though making fun of my replies, and it seemed as if the moment when I could speak to Your Excellency would never come. At last, your Secretary returned to speak to the lady who was with me. He told her that when Your Excellency arrived, she was to make her apologies and take her leave, saying that she had to go elsewhere, since Your Excellency might wish to speak to me in private. I was delighted when I heard this message, and I thought to myself: As His Excellency knows everything, he won't ask me many questions, and he will be alone with me. What a blessing!

When Your Excellency arrived, the good lady played her part very well, and so I had the happiness of speaking with you alone. I am not going to describe now what happened during this interview, because Your Excellency certainly remembers it better than I do. To tell the truth, when I saw Your Excellency receive me with such kindness, without in the least attempting to ask me any useless or curious questions, being concerned solely for the good of my soul, and only too willing to take care of this poor little lamb that the Lord had just entrusted to you, then I was more convinced than ever that Your Excellency did indeed know everything; and I did not hesitate for a moment to give myself completely into your hands. Thereupon, Your Excellency imposed certain conditions which, because of my nature, I found very easy: that is, to keep completely secret all that Your Excellency had said to me, and to be good. I kept my secret to myself, until the day when Your Excellency asked my mother's consent.

Farewell to Fatima

Finally, the day of my departure was settled. The evening before, I went to bid farewell to all the familiar places so dear to us. My heart was torn with loneliness and longing, for I was sure I would never set foot again on the Cabeço, the Rock, Valinhos, or in the parish church where our dear Lord had begun His work of mercy, and the cemetery, where rested the mortal remains of my beloved father and of Francisco, whom I could still never forget. I said goodbye to our well, already illumined by the pale rays of the moon, and to the old threshing-floor where I had so often spent long hours contemplating the beauty of the starlit heavens, and the wonders of sunrise and sunset which so enraptured me. I loved to watch the rays of the sun reflected in the dew drops, so that the mountains seemed covered with pearls in the morning sunshine; and in the evening, after a snowfall, to see the snowflakes sparkling on the pine trees was like a foretaste of the beauties of paradise.

Without saying farewell to anyone, I left the next day [43] at two o'clock in the morning, accompanied by my mother and a poor labourer called Manuel Correia, who was going to Leiria. I carried my secret with me, inviolate. We went by way of the Cova da Iria, so that I could bid it my last farewell. There, for the last time, I prayed my Rosary. As long as this place was still in sight, I kept turning round to say a last goodbye. We arrived at Leiria at nine o'clock in the morning. There I met Dona Filomena Miranda, whom Your Excellency had charged to accompany me. This lady was later to be my godmother at Confirmation. The train left at two o'clock in the afternoon, and there I was at the station, giving my poor mother a last embrace, leaving her overwhelmed with sorrow and shedding abundant tears. The train moved out, and with it went my poor heart plunged in an ocean of loneliness and filled with memories that I could never forget.

EPILOGUE

I think, Your Excellency, that I have just picked the most beautiful flower and the most delicious fruit from my little garden, and I now place it in the merciful hands of the good Lord, whom you represent, praying that he will make it yield a plentiful harvest of souls for eternal life. And since our dear Lord takes pleasure in the humble obedience of the least of His creatures, I end with the words of her whom He, in His infinite mercy, has given me as Mother, Protectress and Model, the very same words with which I began:

«Behold the handmaid of the Lord! May He continue to make use of her, as He thinks best.»

Further Memories of Jacinta

P. S. — I forgot to say that when Jacinta went to hospital in Vila Nova de Ourém and again in Lisbon, she knew she was not going to be cured, but only to suffer. Long before anybody spoke to her of the possibility of her entering the hospital of Vila Nova de Ourém, she said one day:

«Our Lady wants me to go to two hospitals, not to be cured, but to suffer more for love of Our Lord and for sinners.»

I do not know Our Lady's exact words in these apparitions to Jacinta alone, for I never asked her what they were. I confined myself to merely listening to what she occasionally confided to me. In this account, I have tried not to repeat what I have written in the previous one, so as not to make it too long.

Lucia's Magnetic Personality

It may seem perhaps from this account that, in my village, nobody showed me any love or tenderness. But this is not so. There was a dear chosen portion of the Lord's flock, who showed me singular affection. These were the little children. They ran up to me, bubbling over with joy, and when they knew I was pasturing my sheep in the neighbourhood of our little village, whole groups of them used to come and spend the day with me. My mother used to say:

«I don't know what attraction you have for children! They run after you as if they were going to a feast!»

As for myself, I did not feel at ease in the midst of such merriment, and for that reason, I tried to keep out of their way.

The same thing happened to me with my companions in Vilar; and I would almost venture to say that it is happening to me now with my Sisters in religion. A few years ago, I was told by my Mother Mistress, who is now Rev. Mother Provincial:

«You have such an influence over the other Sisters that, if you want to, you can do them a great deal of good.» [44]

And quite recently, Rev. Mother Superior in Pontevedra [45] said to me:

«To a certain degree, you are responsible to Our Lord for the state of fervour or negligence in observance, on the part of the other Sisters, because their fervour is increased or diminished at recreation; whatever the others see you doing at that time, they do as well. Certain topics you brought up at recreation helped other Sisters to understand the Rule better, and made them resolve to observe it more faithfully.»

Why is this?

I don't know. Perhaps it is a talent which the Lord has given me, and for which He will hold me to account. Would that I knew how to trade with it, that I might restore it to Him a thousandfold.

Lucia's Excellent Memory

Maybe someone will want to ask: How can you remember all this? How? I don't know. Our dear Lord, Who shares out His gifts as He thinks fit, has allotted to me this little portion — my memory. He alone knows why. And besides, as far as I can see, there is this difference between natural and supernatural things: «When we are talking to a mere creature, even while we are speaking, we tend to forget what is being said; whereas these supernatural things are ever more deeply engraved on the soul, even as we are seeing and hearing them, so that it is not easy to forget them.»

NOTES: SECOND MEMOIR

1. This was said by the Foundress of the Congregation of Saint Dorothy, Saint Paula Frassinetti.
2. Although the spelling is often faulty, this does not affect the clear and orderly style of Lucia's manuscripts.
3. Luke 1, 48.
4. The names of her brother and sisters are: Maria dos Anjos, Teresa, Manuel, Gloria, Carolina, and another girl who died in infancy.
5. Maria dos Anjos is still living at her parents' home.
6. Lucia was born on March 22nd, 1907.
7. He was identified later with the saintly Father Cruz, S. J., died 1948.
8. This beautiful statue still stands in the Parish Church on the right of the transept.
9. Although at times Lucia's father showed a weakness for wine, he always possessed strong religious convictions.
10. This truly reveals Lucia's simplicity, and still more her candour and honesty in all her writing.
11. This was in the year 1915.
12. The two first — mentioned persons are still living. All three have been interviewed by Fr. Kondor about what Lucia relates here.
13. These indistinct apparitions of the Angel were probably meant to prepare Lucia for the future.
14. This was the first apparition of the Angel, who appeared three times in 1916.
15. The second apparition of the same Angel.
16. The third and last apparition of the same Angel.
17. Some theologians have difficulties regarding this prayer. Two aspects should therefore be taken into account:
    1. It is not necessary to regard this version as verbatim.
    2. This is a form of prayer which was influenced by other popular prayers.
18. Francisco and Jacinta had not yet received their First Communion. However, they never regarded this as a sacramental Communion.
19. His proper name was Fr. Manuel Marques Ferreira. He died in January, 1945.
20. One should not exaggerate her father's conduct. Even if it is true that he liked his wine, he must not be regarded as an alcoholic. As to his religious duties, it is certain that he did not fulfil them in the parish of Fatima for some years, as he did not get along with the priest. However, he did fulfil his Easter duty in Vila Nova de Ourém.
21. These places are situated in the vicinity of Fatima, some as distant as 15 miles.
22. One should note that this was a state of confusion and helplessness, rather than actual doubts, and it was caused by the difficulties in her family, besides the cautious attitude of the priest.
23. The day mentioned as the «following» day was the 11th of August.
24. Dr. Manuel Nunes Formigão Junior, later the great apostle of Fatima, went first to the Cova where the apparitions took place on the 13th of September, and not in August.
25. Lucia mentions here and also elsewhere, that the apparition occurred at Valinhos on August 15th, that is, on the day of her

return from Vila Nova de Ourém. This is a mistake; the day of her return from Ourém was certainly the 15th of August, but the apparition occurred on the following Sunday, 19th of August, 1917.

26. This refers to the visit of Dr. Carlos de Azevedo Mendes on the 8th of September, 1917.

27. We are in possession of the parish priest's valuable report; the same events were brought up during every interrogation.

28. The documents of the period show that one reason for the priest's departure was the difficulty he had to face in connection with the restoration of the church building.

29. Canon Ferreira, priest of Torres Novas at the time, confessed one day that he was one of those troublesome interrogators.

30. This was Father Faustino.

31. The place is called Soutaria. Senhora Emilia's house was rebuilt as a chapel.

32. This property near Torres Novas belonged to the engineer, Mário Godinho. On July 13th, 1917, he himself took the first photograph of the children which we have in our possession.

33. This was certainly not the reason. It was rather the difficulties the priest had with the members of his parish on account of the rebuilding of the church.

34. The date in question is the 13th of May, 1920. These are dates which Lucia could not identify herself.

35. Lucia's father died not on the 31st of July, 1919.

36. Francisco and Jacinta fell ill almost simultaneously, namely towards the end of October, 1918.

37. Francisco died on the 4th of April, 1919, at 10 a.m.

38. Jacinta died on the 20th of February, 1920.

39. Lucia was in Lisbon from the 7th of July to the 6th of August. After that, she went to Santarém, and from there she returned to Aljustrel on the 12th of August.

40. The new Bishop came to the Diocese on the 5th of August, 1920.

41. Fr. Augusto Maia, died 1959.

42. Msgr. Manuel Marques dos Santos, 1892-1971.

43. Lucia left Aljustrel in the early morning of June 16th, 1921, and reached Leiria some hours later. From there, she travelled to the College at Porto, where she arrived the following morning.

44. Madre Maria do Carmo Corte Real.

45. Madre Carmen Refojo, Mother Superior in Pontevedra, 1933-1939.

THIRD MEMOIR

Introduction

We have seen that the two previous Memoirs were written at the suggestion of the Bishop of Leiria and Father Fonseca. This manuscript also was written by Lucia, not on her own initiative but at the request of another person. It happened like this. Two editions of the book «Jacinta» were published, in May and October, 1938, respectively. But when the Silver Jubilee Year of 1942 was drawing near, the publication of a new edition was under consideration. It was felt that Lucia could also make a valuable contribution to this third edition.

The Bishop, Dom José, informed Lucia that Dr. Galamba would visit her, as he wanted to ask her further questions about Jacinta's life. Sister Lucia felt that it would be necessary to disclose the first two parts of the secret of July, 1917, in order to describe the inner life of Jacinta. Therefore, she deemed it essential to make a report on these two parts of the secret, before she could complete her account of Jacinta.

Rev. Dr. Galamba did not meet Lucia on this occasion. She had, however, been thinking about this matter already, as early as the end of the previous July, when the Bishop requested her to write this account. She completed the writing on the 31st of August, and it was sent to the Bishop of Leiria without delay. What Sister Lucia says in the foreword to this account may well be supplemented by the following, which she wrote in her letter to Father Gonçalves:

«His Excellency the Bishop wrote to me about a forthcoming interrogation by Dr. Galamba. He requested me to recall everything I could remember in connection with Jacinta, as a new edition of her life is about to be printed. This request penetrated to the depths of my soul like a ray of light, giving me to know that the time has come to reveal the first two parts of the secret, and thus add two chapters to the new edition: one about hell, and the other about the Immaculate

Heart of Mary. But I am still in doubt, since I am reluctant to reveal the secret. The account has already been completed, but I hesitate as to whether I should send it off or throw it into the fire. I do not know yet what I am going to do.»

The spirit in which Sister Lucia wrote down these reminiscences is the same as in the previous ones: a strong dislike on the one hand, and on the other, a complete obedience which is certain that this is «for the glory of God and for the salvation of souls».

J. M. J.

PROLOGUE

Your Excellency,

In obedience to the order which Your Excellency gave me in your letter of July 26th, 1941, that I should think over and note down anything else I could remember about Jacinta, I have given thought to the matter and decided that, as God was speaking to me through you, the moment has arrived to reply to two questions which have often been sent to me, but which I have put off answering until now.

In my opinion, it would be pleasing to God and to the Immaculate Heart of Mary that, in the book «Jacinta», one chapter would be devoted to the subject of hell, and another to the Immaculate Heart of Mary. [1] Your Excellency will indeed find this opinion rather strange and perhaps inopportune, but it is not my own idea. God Himself will make clear to you that this is a matter that pertains to His glory and to the good of souls.

This will entail my speaking about the secret, and thus answering the first question.

What is the Secret?

What is the secret?

It seems to me that I can reveal it, since I already have permission from heaven to do so. God's representatives on earth have authorised me to do this several times and in various letters, one of which, I believe, is in your keeping. This letter is from Rev. Fr. José Bernardo Gonçalves, [2] and in it he advises me to write to the Holy Father, [3] suggesting, among other things, that I should reveal the secret. I did say something about it. But in order not to make my letter too long, since I was told to keep it short, I confined myself to the essentials, leaving it to God to provide another more favourable opportunity.

In my second account, I have already described in detail the doubt which tormented me from June 13th until July 13th, and how it disappeared completely during the Apparition on that day.

The Vision of Hell

Well, the secret is made up of three distinct parts, two of which I am now going to reveal. [4]

The first part is the vision of hell. [5]

Our Lady showed us a great sea of fire which seemed to be under the earth. Plunged in this fire were demons and souls in human form, like transparent burning embers, all blackened or burnished bronze, floating about in the conflagration, now raised into the air by the flames that issued from within themselves together with great clouds of smoke, now falling back on every side like sparks in a huge fire, without weight or equilibrium, and amid shrieks and groans of pain and despair, which horrified us and made us tremble with fear. The demons could be distinguished by their terrifying and repellent likeness to frightful and unknown animals, all black and transparent. This vision lasted but an instant. How can we ever be grateful enough to our kind heavenly Mother, who had already prepared us by promising, in the first Apparition, to take us to heaven. Otherwise, I think we would have died of fear and terror.

We then looked up at Our Lady, who said to us so kindly and so sadly:

«You have seen hell where the souls of poor sinners go. To save them, God wishes to establish in the world devotion to my Immaculate Heart. [6] If what I say to you is done, many souls will be saved and there will be peace. The war [7] is going to end; but if people do not cease offending God, a worse one will break out during the pontificate of Pius XI. [8] When you see a night illumined by an unknown light, know that this is the great sign [9] given you by God that He is about to punish the world for its crimes, by means of war, famine, and persecutions of the Church and of the Holy Father.

«To prevent this, I shall come [10] to ask for the consecration of Russia to my Immaculate Heart, and the Communion of reparation on the First Saturdays. If my requests are heeded, Russia will be converted, and there will be peace; if not, she will spread her errors throughout the world, causing wars and persecutions of the Church. The good will be martyred; the Holy Father will have much to suffer; various nations will be annihilated. In the end, my Immaculate Heart will triumph. The Holy Father will consecrate Russia to me, [11] and she will be converted, and a period of peace will be granted to the world. [12]

Lasting Impression on Jacinta

Your Excellency, as I already told you in the notes I sent to you after reading the book about Jacinta, some of the things revealed in the secret made a very strong impression on her. This was indeed the case. The vision of hell filled her with horror to such a degree, that every penance and mortification was as nothing in her eyes, if it could only prevent souls from going there.

Well, I am now going to answer the second question, one which has come to me from various quarters.

How is it that Jacinta, small as she was, let herself be possessed by such a spirit of mortification and penance, and understood it so well?

I think the reason is this: firstly, God willed to bestow on her a special grace, through the Immaculate Heart of Mary; and secondly, it was because she had looked upon hell, and had seen the ruin of souls who fall therein.

Some people, even the most devout, refuse to speak to children about hell, in case it would frighten them. Yet God did not hesitate to show hell to three children, one of whom was only six years old, knowing well that they would be horrified to the point of, I would almost dare to say, withering away with fear.

Jacinta often sat thoughtfully on the ground or on a rock, and exclaimed:

«Oh, Hell! Hell! How sorry I am for the souls who go to hell! And the people down there, burning alive, like wood in the fire!» Then, shuddering, she knelt down with her hands joined, and recited the prayer that Our Lady had taught us:

«O my Jesus! Forgive us, save us from the fire of hell. Lead all souls to heaven, especially those who are most in need.»

Now, Your Excellency will understand how my own impression was that the final words of this prayer refer to souls in greatest danger of damnation, or those who are nearest to it. Jacinta remained on her knees like this for long periods of time, saying the same prayer over and over again. From time to time, like someone awaking from sleep, she called out to her brother or myself:

«Francisco! Francisco! Are you praying with me? We must pray very much, to save souls from hell! So many go there! So many!» At other times, she asked: «Why doesn't Our Lady show hell to sinners? If they saw it, they would not sin, so as to avoid going there! You must tell Our Lady to show hell to all the people (referring to those who were in the Cova da Iria at the time of the Apparition). You'll see how they will be converted.»

Afterwards, unsatisfied, she asked me: «Why didn't you tell Our Lady to show hell to those people?»

«I forgot,» I answered.

«I didn't remember either!» she said, looking very sad.

Sometimes, she also asked: «What are the sins people commit, for which they go to hell?»

«I don't know! Perhaps the sin of not going to Mass on Sunday, of stealing, of saying ugly words, of cursing and of swearing.»

«So for just one word, then, people can go to hell?»

«Well, it's a sin!»

«It wouldn't be hard for them to keep quiet, and to go to Mass! I'm so sorry for sinners! If only I could show them hell!»

Suddenly, she would seize hold of me and say:

«I'm going to heaven, but you are staying here. If Our Lady lets you, tell everybody what hell is like, so that they won't commit any more sins and not go to hell.»

At other times, after thinking for a while, she said: «So many people falling into hell! So many people in hell!»

To quieten her, I said: «Don't be afraid! You're going to heaven.»

«Yes, I am,» she said serenely, «but I want all those people to go there too!»

When, in a spirit of mortification, she did not want to eat, I said to her:

«Listen, Jacinta! Come and eat now.»

«No! I'm offering this sacrifice for sinners who eat too much.»

When she was ill, and yet went to Mass on a week day, I urged her:

«Jacinta, don't come! You can't, you're not able. Besides, today is not a Sunday!»

«That doesn't matter! I'm going for sinners who don't go on a Sunday.»

If she happened to hear any of those expressions which some people make a show of uttering, she covered her face with her hands and said:

«Oh, my God, don't those people realize that they can go to hell for saying those things? My Jesus, forgive them and convert them. They certainly don't know that they are offending God by all this! What a pity, my Jesus! I'll pray for them.» There and then, she repeated the prayer that Our Lady had taught us: «Oh, my Jesus, forgive us...»

Lucia Looks Back

Now, Your Excellency, another thought comes to my mind. I have sometimes been asked if, in any of the Apparitions, Our Lady pointed out to us which kind of sins offend God most. They say that Jacinta, when in Lisbon, mentioned sins of the flesh. [13] She had often questioned me on this matter, and I think now, that when in Lisbon, perhaps it occurred to her to put the question to Our Lady herself, and that this was the answer she received.

Well, Your Excellency, it seems to me that I have now made known the first part of the secret.

The Immaculate Heart of Mary

The second part refers to the devotion to the Immaculate Heart of Mary.

As I have already written in the second account, Our Lady told me on June 13th, 1917, that she would never forsake me, and that her Immaculate Heart would be my refuge and the way that would lead me to God. As she spoke these words, she opened her hands, and from them streamed a light that penetrated to our inmost hearts. I think that, on that day, the main purpose of this light was to infuse within us a special knowledge and love for the Immaculate Heart of

Mary, [14] just as on the other two occasions it was intended to do, as it seems to me, with regard to God and the mystery of the most Holy Trinity.

From that day onwards, our hearts were filled with a more ardent love for the Immaculate Heart of Mary. From time to time, Jacinta said to me: «The Lady said that her Immaculate Heart will be your refuge and the way that will lead you to God. Don't you love that? Her Heart is so good! How I love it!»

As I explained earlier, Our Lady told us, in the July secret, that God wished to establish in the world devotion to her Immaculate Heart; and that to prevent a future war, she would come to ask for the consecration of Russia to her Immaculate Heart, and for the Communion of Reparation on the First Saturdays. From then on, whenever we spoke of this among ourselves, Jacinta said: «I am so grieved to be unable to receive Communion in reparation for the sins committed against the Immaculate Heart of Mary!»

I have also mentioned already how Jacinta chose from the litany of ejaculations which Father Cruz suggested to us, this one: «Sweet Heart of Mary, be my salvation!» After saying it, she used to add sometimes, with the simplicity that was natural to her: «I so love the Immaculate Heart of Mary! It is the heart of our dear Mother in heaven! Don't you love saying many times over: 'Sweet Heart of Mary, Immaculate Heart of Mary'? I love it so much, so very much.»

At other times, as she gathered wild flowers, she sang a little tune that she made up herself as she went along: «Sweet Heart of Mary, be my salvation! Immaculate Heart of Mary, convert sinners, save souls from hell!»

Jacinta's Visions of the Holy Father

One day we spent our siesta down by my parents' well. Jacinta sat on the stone slabs on top of the well. Francisco and I climbed up a steep bank in search of wild honey among the brambles in a nearby thicket. After a little while, Jacinta called out to me:

«Didn't you see the Holy Father?»

«No.»

«I don't know how it was, but I saw the Holy Father in a very big house, kneeling by a table, with his head buried in his hands, and he was weeping. Outside the house, there were many people. Some of them were throwing stones, others were cursing him and using bad language. [15] Poor Holy Father, we must pray very much for him.»

I have already told you how, one day, two priests recommended us to pray for the Holy Father, and explained to us who the Pope was. Afterwards, Jacinta asked me:

«Is he the one I saw weeping, the one Our Lady told us about in the secret?» [16]

«Yes, he is,» I answered.

«The Lady must surely have shown him also to those priests. You see, I wasn't mistaken. We need to pray a lot for him.»

At another time, we went to the cave called Lapa do Cabeço. As soon as we got there, we prostrated on the ground, saying the prayers the Angel had taught us. After some time, Jacinta stood up and called to me:

«Can't you see all those highways and roads and fields full of people, who are crying with hunger and have nothing to eat? And the Holy Father in a church praying before the Immaculate Heart of Mary? [17] And so many people praying with him?»

Some days later, she asked me: «Can I say that I saw the Holy Father and all those people?»

«No. Don't you see that that's part of the secret? If you do, they'll find out right away.»

«All right! Then I'll say nothing at all.»

Visions of War

One day, I went to Jacinta's house to spend a little while with her. I found her sitting on her bed, deep in thought.

«Jacinta, what are you thinking about?»

«About the war that is coming. So many people are going to die, and almost all of them are going to hell! [18] Many homes will be destroyed, and many priests will be killed. Look, I am going to heaven, and as for you, when you see the light which the Lady told us would come one night before the war, you run up there too.» [19]

«Don't you see that nobody can just run off to heaven!»

«That's true, you cannot! But don't be afraid! In heaven I'll be praying hard for you, for the Holy Father, for Portugal, so that the war will not come here, [20] and for all priests.»

Your Excellency is not unaware that, a few years ago, God manifested that sign, which astronomers chose to call an aurora borealis. [21] I don't know for certain, but I think if they investigated the matter, they would discover that, in the form in which it appeared, it could not possibly have been an aurora borealis. Be that as it may, God made use of this to make me understand that His justice was about to strike the guilty nations. For this reason, I began to plead insistently for the Communion of Reparation on the First Saturdays, and the consecration of Russia. My intention was to obtain mercy and pardon, not only for the whole world, but for Europe in particular.

When God, in His infinite mercy, made me feel that the terrible moment was drawing near, Your Excellency may recall how, whenever occasion offered, I took the opportunity of pointing it out. I still say that the prayer and penance which have been done in Portugal, have not yet appeased the Divine Justice, for they have not been accompanied by either contrition or amendment. [22] I hope that Jacinta is interceding for us in heaven.

As I said in the notes I sent about the book called «Jacinta», she was most deeply impressed by some of the things revealed to us in the secret. Such was the case with the vision of hell and the ruin of the many souls who go there, or again, the future war with all its horrors, which seemed to be always present to her mind. These made her tremble with fear. When I saw her deep in thought, and asked her: «Jacinta, what are you thinking about?» she frequently replied:

«About the war which is coming, and all the people who are going to die and go to hell! How dreadful! If they would only stop offending God, then there wouldn't be any war and they wouldn't go to hell!»

Sometimes, she also said to me: «I feel so sorry for you! Francisco and I are going to heaven, and you're going to stay here all by yourself! I asked Our Lady to take you to heaven, too, but she wants you to stay here for a while longer. When the war comes, do not be afraid. In heaven, I'll be praying for you.»

Shortly before she went to Lisbon, at one of those times when she felt sad at the thought of our coming separation, I said to her:

«Don't be upset because I can't go with you. You can then spend your time thinking of Our Lady and Our Lord, and saying many times over those words you love so much: 'My God, I love You! Immaculate Heart of Mary, Sweet Heart of Mary', and so on.»

«Yes, indeed,» she eagerly replied, «I'll never get tired of saying those until I die! And then, I can sing them many times over in heaven!»

Lucia Explains her Silence

It may be, Your Excellency, that some people think that I should have made known all this some time ago, because they consider that it would have been twice as valuable years beforehand. [23] This would have been the case, if God had willed to present me to the world as a prophetess. But I believe that God had no such intention, when He made known these things to me. If that had been the case, I think that, in 1917, when He ordered me to keep silence, and this order was confirmed by those who represented Him, [24] He would, on the contrary, have ordered me to speak. I consider then, Your Excellency, that God willed only to make use of me to remind the world that it is necessary to avoid sin, and to make reparation to an offended God, by means of prayer and penance.

Where could I have hidden myself in order to escape from the innumerable questions they would have asked me about such a matter? Even now I am afraid, just thinking of what lies ahead of me! And I must confess that my repugnance in making this known is so great that, although I have before me the letter in which Your Excellency orders me to write everything else that I can remember, and I feel interiorly convinced that this is indeed the hour that God has chosen for my doing this, I still hesitate and experience a real inner conflict, not knowing whether to give you what I have written, or to burn it. As yet, I do not know what will be the outcome of the struggle. It will be as God wills.

For me, keeping silent has been a great grace. What would have happened had I described hell? Being unable to find words which exactly express the reality — for what I say is nothing and gives only a feeble idea of it all — I would therefore have said, now one thing, now another, wanting to explain but not succeeding in doing so. I might thus perhaps have caused such a confusion of ideas as even to spoil, who knows, the work of God. For this reason, I give thanks to the Lord, and I know that He does all things well.

God usually accompanies His revelations with an intimate and detailed understanding of their significance. But I do not venture to speak of this matter, for fear of being led astray, as can all too easily happen, by my own imagination. Jacinta seemed to have this understanding to quite a remarkable degree.

Jacinta and the Immaculate Heart of Mary

A little while before going to hospital, Jacinta said to me:

«It will not be long now before I go to heaven. You will remain here to make known that God wishes to establish in the world devotion to the Immaculate Heart of Mary. When you are to say this, don't go and hide. Tell everybody that God grants us graces through the Immaculate Heart of Mary; that people are to ask her for them; and that the Heart of Jesus wants the Immaculate Heart of Mary to be venerated at His side. Tell them also to pray to the Immaculate Heart of Mary for peace, since God has entrusted it to her. If I could only put into the hearts of all, the fire that is burning within my own heart, and that makes me love the Hearts of Jesus and Mary so very much!» [25]

One day, I was given a holy picture of the Heart of Jesus, quite a nice one, as man-made pictures go. I took it to Jacinta.

«Do you want this holy picture?»

She took it, looked at it attentively, and remarked:

«It's so ugly! It doesn't look like Our Lord at all. He is so beautiful! But I want it; it is He just the same.»

She always carried it with her. At night and during her illness, she kept it under her pillow, until it fell apart. She kissed it frequently, saying:

«I kiss the Heart, because I love it most! How I would love to have a Heart of Mary! Don't you have one? I'd love to have the two together.»

On another occasion, I brought her a picture of a chalice with a host. She took it, kissed it, and radiant with joy she exclaimed:

«It is the Hidden Jesus! I love Him so much! If only I could receive Him in church! Don't they receive Holy Communion in heaven? If they do, then I will go to Holy Commu-

116

nion every day. If only the Angel would go to the hospital to bring me Holy Communion again, how happy I would be!»

Sometimes, on returning from church, I went in to see her, and she asked me:

«Did you receive Holy Communion?»

And if I answered in the affirmative, she said:

«Come over here close to me, for you have the Hidden Jesus in your heart.»

At other times, she told me:

«I don't know how it is! But I feel Our Lord within me. I understand what He says to me, although I neither see Him nor hear Him, but it is so good to be with Him!»

On another occasion, she remarked:

«Look, do you know this? Our Lord is sad, because Our Lady told us not to offend Him any more, for He is already very much offended; yet nobody takes any notice, and they continue to commit the same sins!»

EPILOGUE

There, Your Excellency, is everything else I can remember about Jacinta, and which I don't think I have already said before. The meaning of all I say is exact. [26] As regards the manner of expressing myself, I do not know if I have exchanged one word for another, as for example, when we spoke of Our Lady: sometimes, we said Our Lady, and sometimes, the Lady. And now I no longer remember which of the two phrases we used at a given time. It is the same with a few other small details, which I think are only of minor importance.

I offer to our good God and to the Immaculate Heart of Mary, this little work, which is the fruit of my poor and humble submission to those who represent Him in my regard. I beg Them to make it fruitful for Their glory and the good of souls.

Tuy, 31-8-1941.

1. These chapters were in fact published, not in the second edition (October 1938), but in the third edition (October 1942).
2. Fr. José Bernardo Gonçalves was one of her spiritual directors, died 1966.
3. The letter to Pope Pius XII was dispatched on December 2nd, 1940.
4. It should be noted that it concerns one single secret consisting of three parts. Here, Lucia describes the first two parts. The third part was written at the end of 1943. This part, which has not yet been made public, is in the secret archives of the Vatican.
5. Lucia describes the vision of hell with great realism.
6. In the Message of Fatima, the great promise of the salvation of souls is very often associated with the Immaculate Heart of Mary's intercession.
7. This refers to the First World War, 1914-1918.
8. Lucia has again explicitly confirmed the name of Pope Pius XI. To the objection that the Second World War, 1939-1944, actually started during the Pontificate of Pius XII, she replied that in fact the war began with the occupation of Austria in 1938.
9. Lucia presumed that the «extraordinary» aurora borealis during the night of 25th to 26th of January, 1938, was the sign given by God to announce the imminence of war.
10. This «promise» to come back was fulfilled by the Blessed Virgin on December 10th, 1925, when she appeared to Lucia at Pontevedra (see Appendix 1). On the 13th of June, 1929, Lucia had a further vision at Tuy, when Our Lady asked for the consecration of Russia to her Immaculate Heart.
11. Have the conditions for the consecration of Russia, and consequently for its conversion, as requested by heaven, been complied with? Lucia does not seem to think so. Therefore, we are continuing to suffer from the evils of atheistic communism, a scourge which God uses to punish the world for its sins.
12. This is an unconditional promise, one which will certainly be fulfilled. However, we do not know when it will come true.
13. It is true that Jacinta, on account of her age, did not realize what is meant by this sin. However, this does not mean that, with her great intuition, she did not understand the seriousness of this sin.
14. Jacinta's love for the Immaculate Heart was like an «infused gift», as Lucia tells us, which can only be explained as a great mystic grace bestowed on her.
15. This «vision» of Jacinta about the Holy Father bears great resemblance to the renewal of the consecration of the world to the Immaculate Heart of Mary made by Pius XII in St. Peter's

Basilica on December 8th, 1942, while «outside», that is, in various parts of Europe he was furiously persecuted.

16. This could be a vision of the past as well as of the future. It is to be noted that the year 1917 fell during the Pontificate of Pope Benedict XV. We think, however, that the vision in question points to the future.

17. There is every reason to assume that this refers to Pope Pius XII, the great Pope of the Immaculate Heart of Mary.

18. This is the Second World War. Jacinta experienced this part of the secret in a mystic way.

19. She is undoubtedly exaggerating the terror which such visions inspired in little Jacinta.

20. Although at times in danger, Portugal was actually spared throughout the entire Second World War.

21. See Note 9.

22. Would these words refer to the political and religious events in the Portugal of today, 1974-1976?

23. It could not be said that Lucia's «prophecies» were «post eventum» simply because her superiors released her manuscripts for publication only after the events which had been announced in them. These manuscripts were, in fact, already composed prior to the events taking place.

24. As regards the publication of the documents on Fatima, there was a wonderful «economia silentii», i.e. a special concern which can only be explained by an admirable Divine Providence governing everything that happened.

25. Jacinta's recommendation to promote the devotion to the Immaculate Heart of Mary throughout the world is truly remarkable. For Lucia herself, this was to be a great stimulus in the years to come.

26. It is very important to distinguish between the «meaning» and the «wording», in order to really understand Lucia's manuscripts.

FOURTH MEMOIR

Introduction

This longest of all the Memoirs came into existence like the previous ones, by chance as it were, being written, not on Lucia's own initiative, but at the request of her superiors. On October 7th, 1941, the Bishop of Leiria and Rev. Dr. Galamba, well prepared for further interrogations, came to Valença do Minho, and there Lucia joined them. They brought the Third Memoir with them, explained what Dr. Galamba now desired to know, and presented Dom José's formal request. They so stressed the need for haste that Lucia sent the first note-book to the Bishop, immediately upon its completion, on November 5th. The second and last note-book was finished by the 8th of December.

Now, what was it that was required of Lucia? Someone wanted her to write down absolutely «everything» without delay. But the Bishop very wisely remarked: «No, I will not ask her to do that...». Nevertheless, Lucia was asked to do quite a lot:

1. Dr. Galamba had many questions which, due to lack of time, she was to answer in writing.

2. She was to write down everything she could remember in connection with Francisco, just as she had already done with regard to Jacinta.

3. Further details of the Apparitions of the Angel were requested in writing.

4. She was asked to write a new account of the Apparitions of Our Lady.

5. She was to put in writing any further recollections of Jacinta.

6. The popular songs they sang were to be written down as well.

7. She was to read the book by Fr. Fonseca, and note down everything which she considered inaccurate.

Lucia spared no effort in dealing with all these questions. She answered with admirable clarity and in great detail. She could indeed assure the Bishop: «I believe I have written everything which Your Excellency has asked me to write just now.»

Quite deliberately, she withheld only the third part of the secret. As to the spirit in which she wrote, this does not differ at all from that of her former manuscripts: «...obedience and abandonment to God who works within me. I am truly no more than a poor and miserable instrument which He desires to use, and in a little while, like a painter who casts his now useless brush into the fire so that it may be reduced to ashes, the Divine Artist will Himself reduce His now useless instrument to the ashes of the tomb, until the great day of the eternal Alleluias.»

J. M. J.

PROLOGUE

Confidence and Abandonment

Your Excellency,

After a humble prayer at the feet of Our Lord in the tabernacle and before the Immaculate Heart of Mary, our loving heavenly Mother, asking the grace not to be permitted to write one word, or even a single letter, that is not for Their glory, I come now to begin this work, happy and at peace as are those whose conscience assures them that they are doing in all things the will of God.

Abandoning myself completely into the arms of our heavenly Father and to the protection of the Immaculate Heart of Mary, I therefore once again place in Your Excellency's hands the fruits of my one tree, the tree of obedience.

Inspiration in the Attic

Before making a start, I thought of opening the New Testament, the only book I desire to have here in front of me, in this remote corner of the attic, lit by a single skylight, to which I withdraw whenever I can, in order to escape, as far as possible, from all human eyes. My lap serves as a table, and an old trunk as a chair.

But, someone will say, why don't you write in your cell?

Our dear Lord has seen fit to deprive me even of a cell, although there are quite a few empty ones in the house. [1] As a matter of fact, the community room that we use for work and recreation would seem more suitable for the fulfilment of His designs; but, just as it is inconvenient for writing during the day, so is it all too conducive to drowsiness at night time. But I am glad and I thank God for the grace of having been born poor, and for living more poorly still for love of Him.

Dear Lord! That was not at all what I intended to say.
I must return to what God presented to me when I opened the New Testament.

In St. Paul's Letter to the Philippians 2, 5-8, I read as follows: «Let this mind be in you, which was also in Christ Jesus, who, being in the form of God..., emptied Himself, taking the form of a servant... He humbled Himself, becoming obedient unto death.» After reflecting awhile, I read also verses 12 and 13 of the same chapter: «With fear and trembling work out your salvation. It is God who works in you, both to will and to accomplish, according to His good will.»

Very well then. I need no more than this: obedience and abandonment to God who works within me. I am truly no more than a poor and miserable instrument which He desires to use, and in a little while, like a painter who casts his now useless brush into the fire so that it may be reduced to ashes, the Divine Artist will Himself reduce His now useless instrument to the ashes of the tomb, until the great day of the eternal Alleluias. And I ardently desire that day, for the tomb does not annihilate everything, and the happiness of eternal and infinite love begins — now! [2]

Unction of the Spirit

Your Excellency,

In Valença, on October 7th, 1941, I was asked the following question by Rev. Dr. Galamba:
«Sister, when you said that penance had been done only in part, did you say this of yourself, or was it revealed to you?» I think, Your Excellency, that, in such cases, I never speak or write anything at all that comes from myself alone. I have to thank God for the assistance of the Divine Holy Spirit, whom I feel within me, suggesting to me what I am to write or say. If, at times, my own imagination or understanding suggests something to me, I at once feel the lack of the divine unction, and I stop what I am doing, until I know in my inmost heart what it is that God wants me to say instead. [3] But why do I tell you all this? I do not know. God knows, who has inspired Your Excellency to command me to tell everything, and not deliberately conceal anything.

1. FRANCISCO'S CHARACTER

His Spirituality

I am going to begin then, Your Excellency, by writing what God wills to bring to my mind about Francisco. I hope that Our Lord will make him know in heaven what I am writing about him on earth, so that he may intercede for me with Jesus and Mary, especially during these coming days.

The affection which bound me to Francisco was just one of kinship, [4] and one which had its origin in the graces which heaven deigned to grant us.

Apart from his features and his practice of virtue, Francisco did not seem at all to be Jacinta's brother. Unlike her, he was neither capricious nor vivacious. On the contrary, he was quiet and submissive by nature.

When we were at play and he won the game, if anyone made a point of denying him his rights as winner, he yielded without more ado and merely said: «You think you won? That's alright! I don't mind!»

He showed no love for dancing, as Jacinta did; he much preferred playing the flute while the others danced.

In our games he was quite lively; but few of us liked to play with him as he nearly always lost. I must confess that I myself did not always feel too kindly disposed towards him, as his naturally calm temperament exasperated my own excessive vivacity. Sometimes, I caught him by the arm, made him sit down on the ground or on a stone, and told him to keep still; he obeyed me as if I had real authority over him. Afterwards, I felt sorry, and went and took him by the hand, and he would come along with me as good-humouredly as though nothing had happened. If one of the other children insisted on taking away something belonging to him, he said: «Let them have it! What do I care?»

I recall how, one day, he came to my house and was delighted to show me a handkerchief with a picture of Our Lady of Nazaré on it, which someone had brought him from the seaside. All the children gathered round him to admire it. The handkerchief was passed from hand to hand, and in a few minutes it disappeared. We looked for it, but it was nowhere to be found. A little later, I found it myself in another small boy's pocket. I wanted to take it away from him, but he insisted that it was his own, and that someone had brought him one from the beach as well. To put an end to the quarrel, Francisco then went up to him and said: «Let him have it! What does a handkercief matter to me?» My own opinion is that, if he had lived to manhood, his greatest defect would have been his attitude of «never mind»!

When I was seven and began to take our sheep out to pasture, he seemed to be quite indifferent. In the evenings, he waited for me in my parents' yard, with his little sister, but this was not out of affection for me, but rather to please her. As soon as Jacinta heard the tinkling of the sheep bells, she ran out to meet me; whereas Francisco waited for me, sitting on the stone steps leading up to our front door. Afterwards, he came with us to play on the old threshing floor, while we watched for Our Lady and the Angels to light their lamps. He eagerly counted the stars with us, but nothing enchanted him as much as the beauty of sunrise or sunset. As long as he could still glimpse one last ray of the setting sun, he made no attempt to watch for the first lamp to be lit in the sky.

«No lamp is as beautiful as Our Lord's,» he used to remark to Jacinta, who much preferred Our Lady's lamp because, as she explained, «it doesn't hurt our eyes.» Enraptured, he watched the sun rays glinting on the window panes of the homes in the neighbouring villages, or glistening in the drops of water which spangled the trees and furze bushes of the serra, making them shine like so many stars; in his eyes these were a thousand times more beautiful than the Angels' lamps.

When he persisted in pleading with his mother to let him take care of the flock and therefore come along with me, it was more to please Jacinta than anything else, for she much preferred Francisco's company to that of her brother John. One day his mother, already quite annoyed, refused this permission, and he answered with his usual tranquillity: «Mother, it doesn't matter to me. It's Jacinta who wants me to go.» He confirmed this on yet another occasion. One of my companions came to my house to invite me to go with her, as she had a particularly good pasturage in view for that day. As the sky was overcast, I went to my aunt's house to enquire who was going out that day, Francisco and Jacinta, or their brother John; in case of the latter, I preferred the company of my former companion. My aunt had already decided that, as it looked like rain, John should go. But Francisco went to his mother again, and insisted on going himself. He received a curt and decided «No», whereupon he exclaimed:

«It's all the same with me. It is Jacinta who feels badly about it.»

Natural Inclinations

What Francisco enjoyed most, when we were out on the mountains together, was to perch on the top of the highest rock, and sing or play his flute. If his little sister came down to run races with me, he stayed up there entertaining himself with his music and song. The song he sang most often went like this:

CHORUS

> I love God in heaven,
> I love Him, too, on earth,
> I love the flowers of the fields,
> I love the sheep on the mountains.

> I am a poor shepherd girl,
> I always pray to Mary;
> In the midst of my flock
> I am like the sun at noon.

> Together with my lambkins
> I learn to skip and jump;
> I am the joy of the serra
> And the lily of the vale.

He always took part in our games when we invited him, but he seldom waxed enthusiastic, remarking: «I'll go, but I know I'll be the loser.» These were the games we knew and found most entertaining: pebbles, forfeits, pass the ring, buttons, hit the mark, quoits, and card games such as the bisca game, turning up the kings, queens and knaves, and so on. We had two packs of cards; I had one and they had the other. Francisco liked best to play cards, and the bisca was his favourite game.

Francisco Sees the Angel

During the Apparition of the Angel, he prostrated like his sister and myself, carried away by the same supernatural force that moved us to do so; but he learned the prayer by hearing us repeat it, since, he told us, he heard nothing of what the Angel said.

Afterwards, when we prostrated to say that prayer, he was the first to feel the strain of such a posture; but he remained kneeling, or sitting, and still praying, until we had finished. Later he said: «I am not able to stay like that for a long time, like you. My back aches so much that I can't do it.»

At the second Apparition of the Angel, down by the well, Francisco waited a few moments after it was over, then asked:

«You spoke to the Angel. What did he say to you?»

«Didn't you hear?»

«No. I could see that he was talking to you. I heard what you said to him; but what he said to you, I don't know.»

As the supernatural atmosphere in which the Angel left us, had not yet entirely disappeared, I told him to ask Jacinta or myself next day.

«Jacinta, you tell me what the Angel said.»

«I'll tell you tomorrow. Today I can't talk about it.»

Next day, as soon as he came up to me, he asked me:

«Did you sleep last night? I kept thinking about the Angel, and what he could have said.»

I then told him all that the Angel had said at the first and second Apparitions. But it seemed that he had not received an understanding of all that the words meant, for he asked:

«Who is the Most High? What is the meaning of: 'The Hearts of Jesus and Mary are attentive to the voice of your supplications'?...»

Having received an answer, he remained deep in thought for a while, and then broke in with another question. But my mind was not yet free, so I told him to wait until the next day, because at that moment I was unable to speak. He waited quite contentedly, but he did not let slip the very next opportunity of putting more questions. This made Jacinta say to him:

«Listen! We shouldn't talk much about these things.»

When we spoke about the Angel, I don't know what it was that we felt.

«I don't know how I feel,» Jacinta said. «I can no longer talk, or sing, or play. I haven't strength enough for anything.»

«Neither have I,» replied Francisco, «but what of it? The Angel is more beautiful than all this. Let's think about him.»

In the third Apparition, the presence of the supernatural made itself felt more intensely still. For several days even Francisco did not venture to speak. Later he said:

«I love to see the Angel, but the worst of it is that, afterwards, we are unable to do anything. I couldn't even walk. I don't know what was the matter with me.»

In spite of that, after the third Apparition of the Angel, it was he who noticed that it was getting dark, and who drew our attention to the fact, and thought we should take our flocks back home.

Once the first few days were over and we had returned to normal, Francisco asked:

«The Angel gave you Holy Communion, but what was it that he gave to Jacinta and me?»

It was Holy Communion, too,» replied Jacinta, with inexpressible joy. «Didn't you see that it was the Blood that fell from the Host?»

«I felt that God was within me, but I did not know how!»

Then, prostrating on the ground, he and his sister remained for a long time, saying over and over again the prayer of the Angel «Most Holy Trinity...»

Little by little, the atmosphere of the supernatural faded away, and by the 13th of May, we were playing with almost as much enjoyment and freedom of spirit as we had done before.

Impressions of the First Apparition

The Apparition of Our Lady plunged us once more into the atmosphere of the supernatural, but this time more gently. Instead of that annihilation in the Divine Presence, which exhausted us even physically, it left us filled with peace and expansive joy, which did not prevent us from speaking afterwards of what had happened. However, with regard to the light communicated to us when Our Lady opened her hands, and everything connected with this light, we experienced a kind of interior impulse that compelled us to keep silent.

Afterwards, we told Francisco all that Our Lady had said. He was overjoyed and expressed the happiness he felt when he heard of the promise that he would go to heaven. Crossing his hands on his breast, he exclaimed, «Oh, my dear Our Lady! I'll say as many rosaries as you want!» And from then on, he made a habit of moving away from us, as though going for a walk. When we called him and asked him what he was doing, he raised his hand and showed me his rosary. If we told him to come and play, and say the rosary with us afterwards, he replied:

«I'll pray then as well. Don't you remember that Our Lady said I must pray many rosaries?»

He said to me on one occasion: «I loved seeing the Angel, but I loved still more seeing Our Lady. What I loved most of all was to see Our Lord in that light from Our Lady which penetrated our hearts. I love God so much! But He is very sad because of so many sins! We must never commit any sins again.»

I have already said, in the second account about Jacinta, how he was the one who gave me the news that she had broken our agreement not to say anything. As he shared my opinion that the matter should be kept secret, he added sadly: «As for me, when my mother asked me if it were true, I had to say that it was, so as not to tell a lie.»

From time to time, he said: «Our Lady told us that we would have much to suffer, but I don't mind. I'll suffer all that she wishes! What I want is to go to heaven!»

One day, when I showed how unhappy I was over the persecution now beginning both in my family and outside, Francisco tried to encourage me with these words:

«Never mind! Didn't Our Lady say that we would have much to suffer, to make reparation to Our Lord and to her own Immaculate Heart for all the sins by which They are offended? They are so sad! If we can console them with these sufferings, how happy we shall be!»

When we arrived at our pasturage a few days after Our Lady's first Apparition, he climbed up to the top of a steep rock, and called out to us:

«Don't come up here; let me stay here alone.»

«All right.» And off I went, chasing butterflies with Jacinta. We no sooner caught them than we made the sacrifice of letting them fly away, and we never gave another thought to Francisco. When lunch time came, we missed him and went to call him:

«Francisco, don't you want to come for your lunch?»

«No, you eat.»

«And to pray the Rosary?»

«That, yes, later on. Call me again.»

When I went to call him again, he said to me:

«You come up here and pray with me.»

We climbed up to the peak, where the three of us could scarcely find room to kneel down, and I asked him:

«But what have you been doing all this time?»

«I am thinking about God, Who is so sad because of so many sins! If only I could give Him joy!» [5]

One day, we began to sing in happy chorus about the joys of the serra:

CHORUS

Ah! tra lala, la la
Tra lala, la la
La la la!

In this life everything sings,
And who sings better than I?
The shepherdess out on the serra,
Or the maid a-washing in the stream!

There's the merry chirp of the goldfinch
That comes to awaken me,
As soon as the sun arises,
The brambles come alive with his song.

The screech owl cries at night
Seeking to frighten me,
The girl in the moonlight sings
As she gaily shucks the corn.

The nightingale in the meadow
Spends the whole day long in song,
The turtle dove sings in the wood,
Even the cart squeaks out a song!

The serra is a rock-strewn garden
Smiling happily all the day long,
Sparkling with gleaming dew drops
That glisten on the mountain side!

We sang it right through once, and were about to repeat it, when Francisco interrupted us: «Let's not sing any more. Since we saw the Angel and Our Lady, singing doesn't appeal to me any longer.»

Impressions of the Second Apparition

At the second Apparition on June 13th, 1917, Francisco was deeply impressed by the light which, as I related in the second account, Our Lady communicated to us at the moment when she said: «My Immaculate Heart will be your refuge and the way which will lead you to God.» At the time, he did not seem to grasp the significance of what was happening, perhaps because it was not given to him to hear the accompanying words. For this reason, he asked later:

«Why did Our Lady have a Heart in her hand, spreading out over the world that great light which is God? You were with Our Lady in the light which went down towards the earth, and Jacinta was with me in the light which rose towards heaven!»

«That is because you and Jacinta will soon go to heaven,» I replied, «while I, with the Immaculate Heart of Mary, will remain for some time longer on earth.»

«How many years longer will you stay here?» he asked.

«I don't know. Quite a lot.»

«Was it Our Lady who said so?»

«Yes, and I saw it in the light that she shone into our hearts.»

Jacinta confirmed the very same thing, saying:

«It is just like that! That's exactly how I saw it too!»

He remarked sometimes:

«These people are so happy just because you told them that Our Lady wants the Rosary said, and that you are to learn to read! How would they feel if they only knew what she showed to us in God, in her Immaculate Heart, in that great light! But this is a secret; it must not be spoken about. It's better that no one should know it.»

After this Apparition, whenever they asked us if Our

Lady had said anything else, we began to give this reply: «Yes, she did, but it's a secret.» If they asked us why it was a secret, we shrugged our shoulders, lowered our heads and kept silent. But, after the 13th of July, we said: «Our Lady told us we were not to tell it to anybody,» thus referring to the secret imposed on us by Our Lady.

Francisco Strengthens Lucia's Courage

In the course of this month, the influx of people increased considerably, and so did the constant questionings and contradictions. Francisco suffered quite a lot from all this, and complained to his sister, saying:

«What a pity! If you'd only kept quiet, no one would know! If only it were not a lie, we could tell all the people that we saw nothing, and that would be the end of it. But this can't be done!»

When he saw me perplexed and in doubt, he wept, and said:

«But how can you think that it is the devil? Didn't you see Our Lady and God in that great light? How can we go there without you, when it is you who do the talking?»

That night after supper he came back to my house, called me out to the old threshing floor, and said:

«Look! Aren't you going tomorrow?»

«I'm not going. I've already told you I'm not going back there any more.»

«But what a shame! Why is it that you now think that way? Don't you see that it can't be the devil? God is already sad enough on account of so many sins, and now if you don't go, He'll be sadder still! Come on, say you'll go!»

«I've already told you I'm not going. It's no use asking me.» And I returned abruptly to the house.

A few days later, he said to me: «You know, I never slept at all that night. I spent the whole time crying and praying, begging Our Lady to make you go!»

Impressions of the Third Apparition

In the third Apparition, Francisco seemed to be the one on whom the vision of hell made the least impression, though it did indeed have quite a considerable effect on him. What made the most powerful impression on him and what wholly absorbed him, was God, the Most Holy Trinity, perceived in that light which penetrated our inmost souls. Afterwards, he said:

«We were on fire in that light which is God, and yet we were not burnt! What is God?... We could never put it into words. Yes, that is something indeed which we could never express! But what a pity it is that He is so sad! If only I could console Him!...»

One day, I was asked if Our Lady had told us to pray for sinners, and I said she had not. At the first opportunity, while the people were questioning Jacinta, he called me aside and said:

«You lied just now! How could you say that Our Lady didn't tell us to pray for sinners? Didn't she ask us to pray for sinners, then?»

«For sinners, no! She told us to pray for peace, for the war to end. But for sinners, she told us to make sacrifices.»

«Ah! That's true. I was beginning to think you had lied.»

Francisco in Prison

I have already described how Francisco spent the day praying and weeping, perhaps even more upset than I was, when my father received an order to present me before the Administrator at Vila Nova de Ourém.[6] In prison, he was quite courageous, and tried to cheer up Jacinta when she felt most homesick. While we were saying the Rosary in prison, he noticed that one of the prisoners was on his knees with his cap still on his head. Francisco went up to him and said: «If you wish to pray, you should take your cap off.» Right away, the poor man handed it to him and he went over and put it on the bench on top of his own.

During Jacinta's interrogation, he confided to me with boundless joy and peace: «If they kill us as they say, we'll soon be in heaven! How wonderful! Nothing else matters!» Then after a moment's silence, he added: «God grant that Jacinta won't be afraid. I'm going to say a Hail Mary for her!» He promptly removed his cap and prayed. The guard, seeing him praying, asked him:

«What are you saying?»

«I'm saying a Hail Mary so that Jacinta won't be afraid.»

The guard made a scornful gesture and let him go ahead.

One day, after our return from Vila Nova de Ourém, we began to be aware of the presence of the supernatural all around us, and to feel that we were about to receive some heavenly communication. Francisco at once showed his concern over Jacinta's absence.

«What a pity it would be,» he exclaimed, «if Jacinta did not get here in time!»

He begged his brother to go quickly and get her, adding:

«Tell her to run here.»

After his brother had left us, Francisco said:

«Jacinta will be very sad if she doesn't arrive in time.»

After the Apparition, his sister wanted to stay there the whole afternoon, so he said: «No! You must go home, because Mother didn't let you come out with the sheep.» And to encourage her, he went back to the house with her.

In prison, when we noticed that it was already past midday, and that they would not let us go to the Cova da Iria, Francisco said:

«Perhaps Our Lady will come and appear to us here.»

On the following day, he could not hide his distress, and almost in tears, he said:

«Our Lady must have been very sad because we didn't go to the Cova da Iria, and she won't appear to us again. I would so love to see her!»

While in prison, Jacinta wept bitterly, for she was so homesick for her mother and all the family. Francisco tried to cheer her, saying:

«Even if we never see our mother again, let's be patient! We can offer it for the conversion of sinners. The worst thing would be if Our Lady never came back again! That is what hurts me most. But I offer this as well for sinners.»

Afterwards, he asked me:

«Tell me! Will Our Lady not come and appear to us any more?»

«I don't know. I think she will.»

«I miss her so much!»

The Apparition at Valinhos was, therefore, a double joy for him. He had been tormented by the fear that she would never return. He told me later:

«Most likely, she didn't appear on the 13th, so as to avoid going to the Administrator's house, maybe because he is such a bad man.»

Impressions of the Last Apparitions

After the 13th of September, when I told Francisco that in October Our Lord would come as well, he was overwhelmed with joy. «Oh, how good He is! I've only seen Him twice, and I love Him so much!» [7] From time to time, he asked:

«Are there many days left till the 13th? I'm longing for that day to come, so that I can see Our Lord again.» Then he thought for a moment, and added:

«But listen! Will He still be so sad? I am so sorry to see Him sad like that! I offer Him all the sacrifices I can think of. Sometimes, I don't even run away from all those people, just in order to make sacrifices!»

After October 13th, he said to me:

«I loved seeing Our Lord, but I loved still more seeing Him in that light where we were with Him as well. It's not long now, and Our Lord will take me up close to Him, and then I can look at Him forever.»

One day, I asked him:

«When you are questioned, why do you put your head down and not want to answer?»

«Because I want you to answer, and Jacinta too. I didn't hear anything. I can only say that I saw. Then, supposing I said something you don't want me to say?»

Every now and then, he went off and left us without warning. When we missed him, we went in search of him, calling out his name. He answered from behind a little wall, or a shrub or a clump of brambles, and there he was on his knees, praying.

«Why didn't you tell us so that we could come and pray with you?»

«Because I prefer to pray alone.»

In my notes on the book called «Jacinta», I've already related what happened on a piece of land known as Varzea. I don't think I need to repeat it here.

On our way to my home one day, we had to pass by my godmother's house. She had just been making a mead drink, and called us in to give us a glass. We went in, and Francisco was the first to whom she offered a glassful. He took it, and without drinking it, he passed it on to Jacinta, so that she and I could have a drink first. Meanwhile, he turned on his heel and disappeared.

«Where is Francisco?» my godmother asked.

«I don't know! He was here just now.»

He did not return, so Jacinta and I thanked my godmother for the drink and went in search of Francisco. We knew beyond a shadow of a doubt that he would be sitting on the edge of the well which I have mentioned so often.

«Francisco, you didn't drink your glass of mead! My godmother called you so many times, and you didn't appear!»

«When I took the glass, I suddenly remembered I could offer that sacrifice to console Our Lord, so while you two were taking a drink, I ran over here.»

Anecdotes and Popular Songs

Between my house and Francisco's lived my godfather Anastacio, who was married to an older woman whom God had not blessed with children. They were farmers and quite well-off, so they didn't need to work. My father was overseer of their farm and had charge of the day labourers. In gratitude for this, they showed a special liking for me, particularly my godfather's wife, whom I called my godmother Teresa. If I didn't call in during the day, I had to go and sleep there at night, because she couldn't get along without her little «sweetmeat», as she called me.

On festive occasions, she delighted in dressing me up with her gold necklace and heavy earrings which hung down below my shoulders, and a pretty little hat decorated with immense feathers of different colours and fastened with an array of gold beads. At the «festas», there was no one better turned out than I, and how my sisters and my godmother gloried in the fact! The other children crowded round me to admire the brilliance of my finery. To tell the truth, I myself greatly enjoyed the «festa», and vanity was my worst adornment. Everybody showed liking and esteem for me, except a poor orphan girl whom my godmother Teresa had taken into her home on the death of her mother. She seemed to fear that I would get part of the inheritance she was hoping for, and indeed she would not have been mistaken, had not Our Lord destined for me a far more precious inheritance.

As soon as the news of the Apparitions got around, my godfather showed unconcern, and my godmother was completely opposed to it all. She made no secret of her disapproval of such «inventions», as she called them. I began, therefore, to keep away from her house as much as I could.

My disappearance was soon followed by that of the groups of children who so often gathered there, and whom my godmother loved to watch singing and dancing. She treated them to dried figs, nuts, almonds, chestnuts, fruit, and so on.

One Sunday afternoon, I was passing near her house with Francisco and Jacinta, when she called out to us: «Come in, my little swindlers, come! You've not been here for a long time!» Once inside, she lavished her usual attentions on us. The other children seemed to guess we were there, and began to come along as well. My kind godmother, happy at seeing us all gathered in her house once again after such a long space of time, heaped delicacies upon us, and wanted to see us sing and dance.

«Come on,» we said, «what will it be, this one, or that?»

My godmother made the choice herself. It was «Congratulations without illusions», a part song for boys and girls:

CHORUS

You are the sun of the sphere,
Do not deny it your rays!
These are the smiles of springtime,
Ah! change them not into sighs!

Congratulations to the maiden,
Fragrant as the dewy dawn,
Smiling, you anticipate
The caressing of another morn.

The year is rich in flowers,
Rich in fruits and every good!
And may the year that dawns
Be rich in hopes for you!

These hopes are the best of gifts,
Our warmest wishes for you!
Place them upon your brow,
They're the finest crown of all!

If the past was lovely,
The future will be so too!
Greetings for the year now gone,
For the year to come as well!

In this merry banquet of life,
Charming Atlantic flower,
The gardener and the garden fair
Are lauded in gladsome song!

Your heart is yearning for the flowers
That bloom on your native soil,
For your home and its purest loves
That entwine around your heart!

11.

CHORUS

Do you think it right, good sir,
When the topsail veers in sight,
That Berlenga and the Carvoeiro [8]
— Ah! —
Extinguish their lighthouse beams?

But the sea is lashed to fury:
An everlasting swirling main!
Each night is a howling turmoil
That leads to a watery grave.

Gloomy sandbanks of Papoa, [8]
Estelas and Farilhões!
What tragedy ever re-echoes
In the crash of the foaming waves!

Each rugged reef in these waters
Is a grim presage of death!
Every wave chants a doleful dirge
Each cross recalls a wreck!

Then, how can you be so cruel
And put out your light that is life
Way out on the darkened waters
Guiding boats securely ashore.

111.

I no longer shed any tears
When I speak of our farewell,
My hesitating took but a moment
— Ah! —
My loss lasts all life through.

Go and tell heaven to arrest
The flowing torrent of its grace,
Let the flowers wilt and wither
They no longer bespeak your care.

Go, I am too disconsolate,
My sanctuary all in mourning,
High up in the towering steeple
The bronze bell tolls out death.

But you leave me sad and lonely
In the churchyard grey and grim,
Carved out on the black of your tombstone
I leave my eternal laments.

This garden today is so bare,
But once all smiling and gay,
No care did it lack before,
'Twas the gardener who left it to die.

I trust in Providence bestowing
Tender caresses to come!
Hopefully prepared for everyone,
All who leave the homely nest.

Francisco, the Little Moralist

The women of the neighbourhood no sooner heard the
lively singing than they came over to join us, and at the end
they asked us to sing it through again. Francisco, however,
came up to me and said: «Let's not sing that song any more.
Our Lord certainly does not want us to sing things like that

now.» We therefore slipped away among the other children, and ran off to our favourite well.

To tell the truth, now that I have just finished writing out the song under obedience, I cover my face with shame. But Your Excellency, at the request of Rev. Dr. Galamba, has seen fit to order me to write down the popular songs that we knew. Here they are then! I do not know why they are wanted, but for me it is enough to know that I am thus fulfilling God's will.

Meanwhile, it was getting near Carnival time, in 1918. The boys and girls met once again that year to prepare the usual festive meals and fun of those days. Each one brought something from home — such as olive oil, flour, meat, and so on — to one of the houses, and the girls then did the cooking for a sumptuous banquet. All those three days, feasting and dancing went on well into the night, above all on the last day of the Carnival.

The children under fourteen had their own celebration in another house. Several of the girls came to ask me to help them organize our «festa». At first, I refused. But finally, I gave in like a coward, especially after hearing the pleading of José Carreira's sons and daughter, for it was he who had placed his home in Casa Velha at our disposal. He and his wife insistently asked me to go there. I yielded then, and went with a crowd of youngsters to see the place. There was a fine large room, almost as big as a hall, which was well suited for the amusements, and a spacious yard for the supper! Everything was arranged, and I came home, outwardly in most festive mood, but inwardly with my conscience protesting loudly. As soon as I met Jacinta and Francisco, I told them what had happened.

«Are you going back again to those parties and games?» Francisco asked me sternly. «Have you already forgotten that we promised never to do that any more?»

«I didn't want to go at all. But you can see how they never stopped begging me to go; and now I don't know what to do!»

There was indeed no end to the entreaties, nor to the number of girls who came insisting that I play with them. Some even came from far distant villages — from Moita came Rosa, Ana Caetano and Ana Brogueira; from Fatima, the two daughters of Manuel Caracol; from Boleiros, the two daughters of Manuel da Ramira, and two of Joaquim

Chapeleta as well; from Amoreira, the two Silva girls; from Currais, Laura Gato, Josefa Valinho, and several others whose names I have forgotten; besides those who came from Boleiros and Lomba de Pederneira, and so on; and this quite apart from all those who came from Eira da Pedra, Casa Velha, and Aljustrel. How could I so suddenly let down all those girls, who seemed not to know how to enjoy themselves without my company, and make them understand that I had to stop going to these gatherings once and for all? God inspired Francisco with the answer:

«Do you know how you could do it? Everybody knows that Our Lady has appeared to you. Therefore, you can say that you have promised her not to dance any more, and for this reason you are not going! Then, on such days, we can run away and hide in the cave on the Cabeço. Up there nobody will find us!»

I accepted his proposal, and once I had made my decision, nobody else thought of organizing any such gathering. God's blessing was with us. Those friends of mine, who until then sought me out to have me join in their amusements, now followed my example, and came to my home on Sunday afternoons to ask me to go with them to pray the Rosary in the Cova da Iria.

Francisco, Lover of Solitude and Prayer

Francisco was a boy of few words. Whenever he prayed or offered sacrifices, he preferred to go apart and hide, even from Jacinta and myself. Quite often, we surprised him hidden behind a wall or a clump of blackberry bushes, whither he had ingeniously slipped away to kneel and pray, or «think», as he said, «of Our Lord, Who is sad on account of so many sins.»

If I asked him: «Francisco, why don't you tell me to pray with you, and Jacinta too?»

«I prefer praying by myself,» he answered, «so that I can think and console Our Lord, Who is so sad!»

I asked him one day:

«Francisco, which do you like better — to console Our Lord, or to convert sinners, so that no more souls will go to hell?»

«I would rather console Our Lord. Didn't you notice how sad Our Lady was that last month, when she said that people must not offend Our Lord any more, for He is already much offended? I would like to console Our Lord, and after that, convert sinners so that they won't offend Him any more.»

Sometimes, on our way to school, as soon as we reached Fatima, he would say to me:

«Listen! You go to school, and I'll stay here in the church, close to the Hidden Jesus. It's not worth my while learning to read, as I'll be going to heaven very soon. On your way home, come here and call me.»

The Blessed Sacrament was kept at that time near the entrance of the church, on the left side, as the church was undergoing repairs. [9] Francisco went over there, between the baptismal font and the altar, and that was where I found him on my return.

Later, when he fell ill, he often told me, when I called in to see him on my way to school: «Look! Go to the church and give my love to the Hidden Jesus. What hurts me most is that I cannot go there myself and stay awhile with the Hidden Jesus.»

When I arrived at his house one day, I said goodbye to a group of school children who had come with me, and I went in to pay a visit to him and his sister. As he had heard all the noise, he asked me:

«Did you come with all that crowd?»

«Yes, I did.»

«Don't go with them, because you might learn to commit sins. When you come out of school, go and stay for a little while near the Hidden Jesus, and afterwards come home by yourself.»

On one occasion, I asked him:

«Francisco, do you feel very sick?»

«I do, but I'm suffering to console Our Lord.»

When Jacinta and I went into his room one day, he said to us:

«Don't talk much today, as my head aches so badly.»

«Don't forget to make the offering for sinners,» Jacinta reminded him.

«Yes. But first I make it to console Our Lord and Our Lady, and then, afterwards, for sinners and for the Holy Father.»

On another occasion, I found him very happy when I arrived.

«Are you better?»

«No. I feel worse. It won't be long now till I go to heaven. When I'm there, I'm going to console Our Lord and Our Lady very much. Jacinta is going to pray a lot for sinners, for the Holy Father and for you. You will stay here, because Our Lady wants it that way. Listen, you must do everything that she tells you.»

While Jacinta seemed to be solely concerned with the one thought of converting sinners and saving souls from going to hell, Francisco appeared to think only of consoling Our Lady, who had seemed to him to be so sad.

Francisco Sees the Devil

How different is the incident that I now call to mind. One day we went to a place called Pedreira, and while the sheep were browsing, we jumped from rock to rock, making our voices echo down in the deep ravines. Francisco withdrew, as was his wont, to a hollow among the rocks.

A considerable time had elapsed, when we heard him shouting and crying out to us and to Our Lady. Distressed lest something might have happened to him, we ran in search of him, calling out his name.

«Where are you?»

«Here! Here!»

But it still took us some time before we could locate him. At last, we came upon him, trembling with fright, still on his knees, and so upset that he was unable to rise to his feet.

«What's wrong? What happened to you?»

In a voice half smothered with fright, he replied:

«It was one of those huge beasts that we saw in hell. He was right here breathing out flames!»

I saw nothing, neither did Jacinta, so I laughed and said to him:

«You never want to think about hell, so as not to be afraid; and now you're the first one to be frightened!»

Indeed, whenever Jacinta appeared particularly moved by the remembrance of hell, he used to say to her:

«Don't think so much about hell! Think about Our Lord and Our Lady instead. I don't think about hell, so as not to be afraid.»

He was anything but fearful. He'd go anywhere in the dark alone at night, without the slightest hesitation. He played with lizards, and when he came across any snakes he got them to entwine themselves round a stick, and even poured sheep's milk into the holes in the rocks for them to drink. He went hunting for foxes' holes and rabbits' burrows, for genets, and other creatures of the wilds.

Francisco and His Feathered Friends

Francisco was very fond of birds, and could not bear to see anyone robbing their nests. He always kept part of the bread he had for his lunch, breaking it into crumbs and spreading them out on top of the rocks, so that the birds could eat them. Moving away a little, he called them, as though he expected them to understand him. He didn't want anyone else to approach, lest they be frightened.

«Poor wee things! You are hungry,» he said, as though conversing with them. «Come, come and eat!»

And they, keen-eyed as they are, did not wait for the invitation, but came flocking around him. It was his delight to see them flyng back to the tree tops with their little craws full, singing and chirping in a deafening chorus, in which Francisco joined with rare skill.

One day we met a little boy carrying in his hand a small bird that he had caught. Full of compassion, Francisco promised him two coins, if only he would let the bird fly away. The boy readily agreed. But first he wished to see the money in his hand. Francisco ran all the way home from the Carreira pond, which lies a little distance below the Cova da Iria, to fetch the coins, and so let the little prisoner free. Then, as he watched it fly away, he clapped his hands for joy, and said: «Be careful! Don't let yourself be caught again.»

Thereabouts, lived an old woman called Ti Maria Carreira, whose sons sent her out sometimes to take care of their flock of goats and sheep. The animals were rather wild, and often strayed away in different directions. Whenever we met Ti Maria in these straits, Francisco was the first to run to her aid. He helped her to lead the flock to pasture, chased after the stray ones and gathered them all together again. The poor old woman overwhelmed Francisco with her thanks and called him her dear guardian angel.

When we came across any sick people, he was filled with compassion and said: «I can't bear to see them, as I feel so sorry for them! Tell them I'll pray for them.»

One day, they wanted to take us to Montelo to the home of a man called Joaquim Chapeleta. Francisco did not want to go. «I'm not going, because I can't bear to see people who want to speak and cannot.» (This man's mother was dumb).

When Jacinta and I returned home at nightfall, I asked my aunt where Francisco was.

«How do I know!» she replied. «I'm worn out looking for him all afternoon. Some ladies came and wanted to see you. But you two were not here. He vanished, and never appeared again. Now you go and look for him!»

We sat down for a bit on a bench in the kitchen, thinking that we would go later to the Loca do Cabeço, certain that we would find him there. But no sooner had my aunt left the house, than his voice came from the attic through a little hole in the ceiling. He had climbed up there when he thought that some people were coming. From this vantage point he had observed everything that happened, and told us afterwards:

«There were so many people! Heaven help me if they had ever caught me by myself! What ever would I have said to them?»

(There was a trap-door in the kitchen, which was easily reached by placing a chair on a table, thus affording access to the attic.)

Francisco's Love and Zeal

As I have already said, my aunt sold her flock before my mother disposed of ours. From then onwards, before I went out in the morning, I let Jacinta and Francisco know the place where I was going to pasture the sheep that day; as soon as they could get away, they came to join me.

One day, they were waiting for me when I arrived.

«Oh! How did you get here so early?»

«I came,» answered Francisco, «because — I don't know why — being with you didn't matter much to me before, and I just came because of Jacinta; but now, I can't sleep in the morning as I'm so anxious to be with you.»

Once the Apparitions on each 13th of the month were over, he said to us on the eve of every following 13th:

«Look! Early tomorrow morning, I'm making my escape out through the back garden to the cave on the Cabeço. As soon as you can, come and join me there.»

Oh dear! There I was, writing things about his being sick and near to death, and now I see that I have gone back to the happy times we had on the serra, with the birds chirping merrily all around us. I ask your forgiveness. In writing down what I can remember, I am like a crab that walks backwards and forwards without bothering about reaching the end of its journey. I leave my work to Dr. Galamba, in case he can make use of anything in it, though I suppose he will find little or nothing.

I return, therefore, to Francisco's illness. But, first, I will tell you something about his brief schooling. He came out of the house one day and met me with my sister Teresa, who was already married and living in Lomba. Another woman from a nearby hamlet had asked her to come to me about her son who had been accused of some crime which I no longer remember, and if he could not prove his innocence he was to be condemned, either to exile or to a term of some years imprisonment. Teresa asked me insistently, in the name of the poor woman for whom she wished to do such a favour, to plead for this grace with Our Lady. Having received the message, I set out for school, and on the way, I told my cousins all about it. When we reached Fatima, Francisco said to me:

«Listen! While you go to school, I'll stay with the Hidden Jesus, and I'll ask Him for that grace.»

When I came out of school, I went to call him and asked:

«Did you pray to Our Lord to grant that grace?»

«Yes, I did. Tell your Teresa that he'll be home in a few days' time.»

And indeed, a few days later, the poor boy returned home. On the 13th, he and his entire family came to thank Our Lady for the grace they had received.

On another occasion I noticed, as we left the house, that Francisco was walking very slowly:

«What's the matter?» I asked him. «You seem unable to walk!»

«I've such a bad headache, and I feel as though I'm going to fall.»

«Then don't come. Stay at home!»

«I don't want to. I'd rather stay in the church with the Hidden Jesus, while you go to school.»

Francisco was already sick, but could still manage to walk a little, so one day I went with him to the cave on the Cabeço, and to Valinhos. On our return home, we found the house full of people. A poor woman was standing near a table, pretending to bless innumerable pious objects: rosary beads, medals, crucifixes and so on. Jacinta and I were soon surrounded by a crowd of people who wanted to question us. Francisco was seized upon by the would-be «blesser», who invited him to help her.

«I could not give a blessing,» he replied very seriously, «and neither should you! Only priests do that.»

The little boy's words went round the crowd like lightning, as though spoken by some loud-speaker, and the poor woman had to make a quick departure amid a hail of insults from the people, all demanding back the objects they had just handed over to her.

I already related in my account of Jacinta, how he managed to go one day to the Cova da Iria; how he wore the rope and then handed it back to me; how he was the first, on a day when the heat was suffocating, to offer the sacrifice of not taking a drink; and how he sometimes reminded his sister about suffering for sinners, and so on. I presume, therefore, that it is not necessary to repeat these things here.

One day, I was by his bedside, keeping him company. Jacinta, who had got up for a while, was there too. Suddenly, his sister Teresa came to warn us that a veritable multitude of people were coming down the road, and were obviously looking for us. As soon as she had gone out, I said to Francisco: «Alright! You two wait for them here. I'm going to hide.»

Jacinta managed to run out behind me, and we both succeeded in concealing ourselves inside a barrel which was overturned just outside the door leading to the back garden. It was not long before we heard the noise of people searching the house, going out through the garden and even standing right beside the barrel; but we were saved by the fact that its open end was turned in the opposite direction.

When we felt that they had all gone away, we came out of our hiding place, and went to rejoin Francisco, who told us all that had happened.

«There were so many people and they wanted me to tell them where you were, but I didn't know myself. They wished to see us and ask us lots of things. Besides that, there was a woman from Alqueidão, who wanted the cure of a sick person and the conversion of a sinner. I'll pray for that woman, and you pray for the others — there's such a lot of them.»

Shortly after Francisco's death, this woman came to see us, and asked me to show her his grave. She wished to go there and thank him for the two graces for which she had asked him to pray.

One day, we were just outside Aljustrel, on our way to the Cova da Iria, when a group of people came upon us by surprise around the bend in the road. In order the better to see and hear us, they set Jacinta and myself on top of a wall. Francisco refused to let himself be put there, as though he were afraid of falling. Then, little by little, he edged his way out and leaned against a dilapidated wall on the opposite side. A poor woman and her son, seeing that they could not manage to speak to us personally, as they wished, went and knelt down in front of Francisco. They begged him to obtain from Our Lady the grace that the father of the family would be cured and that he would not have to go to the war. Francisco knelt down also, took off his cap and asked if they would like to pray the Rosary with him. They said they would, and began to pray. Very soon, all those people stopped asking curious questions, and also went down on their knees to pray. After that, they went with us to the Cova da Iria, reciting a Rosary along the way. Once there, we said another Rosary, and then they went away, quite happy.

The poor woman promised to come back and thank Our Lady for the graces she had asked for, if they were granted. She came back several times, accompanied not only by her son but also her husband, who had by now recovered. They came from the parish of S. Mamede, and we called them the Casaleiros.

Francisco's Illness

While he was ill, Francisco always appeared joyful and content. I asked him sometimes:

«Are you suffering a lot, Francisco?»

«Quite a lot, but never mind! I am suffering to console Our Lord, and afterwards, within a short time, I am going to heaven!»

«Once you get there, don't forget to ask Our Lady to take me there soon as well.»

«That, I won't ask! You know very well that she doesn't want you there yet.»

The day before he died, he said to me:

«Look! I am very ill; it won't be long now before I go to heaven.»

«Then listen to this. When you're there, don't forget to pray a great deal for sinners, for the Holy Father, for me and for Jacinta.»

«Yes, I'll pray. But look, you'd better ask Jacinta to pray for these things instead, because I'm afraid I'll forget when I see Our Lord. And then, more than anything else I want to console Him.»

One day, early in the morning, his sister Teresa came looking for me.

«Come quickly to our house! Francisco is very bad, and says he wants to tell you something.»

I dressed as fast as I could and went over there. He asked his mother and brothers and sisters to leave the room, saying that he wanted to ask me a secret. They went out, and he said to me:

«I am going to confession so that I can receive Holy Communion, and then die. I want you to tell me if you have seen me commit any sin, and then go and ask Jacinta if she has seen me commit any.»

«You disobeyed your mother a few times,» I answered, «when she told you to stay at home, and you ran off to be with me or to go and hide.»

«That's true. I remember that. Now go and ask Jacinta if she remembers anything else.»

I went, and Jacinta thought for a while, then answered:

«Well, tell him that, before Our Lady appeared to us, he stole a coin from our father to buy a music box from José Marto of Casa Velha; and when the boys from Aljustrel threw stones at those from Boleiros, he threw some too!»

When I gave him this message from his sister, he answered:

«I've already confessed those, but I'll do so again. Maybe, it is because of these sins that I committed that Our Lord is so sad! But even if I don't die, I'll never commit them again. I'm heartily sorry for them now.» Joining his hands, he recited the prayer: «O my Jesus, forgive us, save us from the fire of hell, lead all souls to heaven, especially those who are most in need.»

Then he said: «Now listen, you must also ask Our Lord to forgive me my sins.»

«I'll ask that, don't worry. If Our Lord had not forgiven them already, Our Lady would not have told Jacinta the other day that she was coming soon to take you to heaven. Now, I'm going to Mass, and there I'll pray to the Hidden Jesus for you.»

«Then, please ask Him to let the parish priest give me Holy Communion.»

«I certainly will.»

When I returned from the church, Jacinta had already got up and was sitting on his bed. As soon as Francisco saw me, he asked:

«Did you ask the Hidden Jesus that the parish priest would give me Holy Communion?»

«I did.»

«Then, in heaven, I'll pray for you.»

«You will? The other day, you said you wouldn't!»

«That was about taking you there very soon. But if you want me to pray for that, I will, and then let Our Lady do as she wishes.»

«Yes, do. You pray.»

«Alright. Don't worry, I'll pray.»

Then I left them, and went off to my usual daily tasks of lessons and work. When I came home at night, I found him radiant with joy. He had made his confession, and the parish priest had promised to bring him Holy Communion next day.

On the following day, after receiving Holy Communion, he said to his sister:

«I am happier than you are, because I have the Hidden Jesus within my heart. I'm going to heaven, but I'm going to pray very much to Our Lord and Our Lady for them to bring you both there soon.»

Jacinta and I spent almost the whole of that day at his bedside. As he was already unable to pray, he asked us to pray the Rosary for him. Then he said to me:

«I am sure I shall miss you terribly in heaven. If only Our Lady would bring you there soon, also!»

«You won't miss me! Just imagine! And you right there with Our Lord and Our Lady! They are so good!»

«That's true! Perhaps, I won't remember!»

Then I added: «Perhaps you'll forget! But never mind!»

Francisco's Holy Death

That night I said goodbye to him.

«Goodbye, Francisco! If you go to heaven tonight, don't forget me when you get there, do you hear me?»

«No, I wont forget. Be sure of that.» Then, seizing my right hand, he held it tightly for a long time, looking at me with tears in his eyes.

«Do you want anything more?» I asked him, with tears running down my cheeks too.

«No!» he answered in a low voice, quite overcome.

As the scene was becoming so moving, my aunt told me to leave the room.

«Goodbye then, Francisco! Till we meet in heaven, goodbye!...»

Heaven was drawing near. He took his flight to heaven the following day in the arms of his heavenly Mother. [10] I could never describe how much I missed him. This grief was a thorn that pierced my heart for years to come. It is a memory of the past that echoes forever unto eternity.

'Twas night: I lay peacefully dreaming
That on this festive longed-for day
Of heavenly union, the Angels above
Vied with us here in holy emulation!

What golden crown beyond all telling,
What garland of flowers garnered here below
Could equal the crown heaven was offering
Angelic beauty, all earthly longing stilled.

The joy, the smile, of our loving Mother...
In the heavenly realms, he lives in God,
Ravished with love, with joys surpassing,
Those years on earth were so swift, so fleeting...
                                        Farewell!

Popular Songs

As Dr. Galamba has asked for the words of popular songs, I have already written some of them in the course of my account of Francisco. Before I embark on another subject, I am going to put down some more of these songs here, so that His Reverence may choose among them, if perchance he may be able to make use of them for whatever purpose he has in mind.

THE MOUNTAIN MAID

Mountain maid, mountain maid,
With eyes of chestnut hue,
Who gave you, sweet mountain maid
Such charms beyond compare?
Such charms beyond compare!
I've never seen the like!

> Mountain maid, mountain maid,
> Look kindly on me,
> Look kindly on me,
> Mountain maid, mountain maid,
> Look kindly on me!

Mountain maid, mountain maid,
With billowing skirt,
How come, sweet mountain maid,
So elegant you are,
So elegant you are,
I've never seen the like!

(Repeat chorus as above)

Mountain maid, mountain maid,
In the rosy flush of youth
Who gave you, sweet mountain maid
That bloom beyond compare,
That bloom beyond compare,
I've never seen the like!

(Chorus)

Mountain maid, mountain maid,
All bedecked in gold,
Who gave you, sweet mountain maid
Your gaily twirling skirt,
Your gaily twirling skirt,
I've never seen the like!

(Chorus)

152

TAKE CARE

If you go up to the serra,
Go with easy tread!
Take care not to lose your foothold
And fall down a deep ravine,
And fall down a deep ravine.
Indeed I could never tumble,
For all the mountain lasses
Will come flocking to my aid,
Will come flocking to my aid.
Whether you will it, or will it not
Sweet lasses, my heart's all yours!

They'll come flocking to my aid,
They'll take good care of me:
Merry mountain lasses,
How good it is to love you,
How good it is to love you,
Whether you will it, or will it not,
Sweet lasses, my heart's all yours!

11. THE STORY OF THE APPARITIONS

PROLOGUE

Now, Your Excellency, we come to the most difficult part of all that you have commanded me to put in writing. First of all, Your Excellency has expressly required of me to write about the Apparitions of the Angel, putting down every circumstance and detail, and even, as far as possible, their interior effects upon us. Then, along comes Dr. Galamba to ask you to command me also to write about the Apparitions of Our Lady.

«Command her, Your Excellency,» he said a little while ago in Valença. «Yes, Your Excellency, command her to write everything, absolutely everything. She'll have to do the rounds of purgatory many a time for having kept silent about so many things!»

As for purgatory, I am not in the least afraid of it, from this point of view. I have always obeyed, and obedience deserves neither penalty nor punishment. Firstly, I obeyed the interior inspirations of the Holy Spirit, and secondly, I obeyed the commands of those who spoke to me in His name. This very thing was the first order and counsel which God deigned to give me through Your Excellency. Happy and content, I recalled the words I had heard long ago from the lips of that holy priest, the Vicar of Torres Novas: «The secret of the King's daughter should remain hidden in the depths of her heart.» Then, beginning to penetrate their meaning, I said: «My secret is for myself». But now, I can no longer say so. Immolated on the altar of obedience, I say rather: «My secret belongs to God. I have placed it in His hands; may He do with it as best pleases Him.»

Dr. Galamba said then: «Your Excellency, command her to say everything, everything, and to hide nothing.» And Your Excellency, assisted most certainly by the Holy Spirit, pronounced this judgement: «No, I will not command that! I will have nothing to do with matters of secrets.» [1]

Thanks be to God! Any other order would have been for me a source of endless perplexities and scruples. Had I received a contrary command, I would have asked myself, times without number: «Whom should I obey? God or His representative?» And perhaps, being unable to come to a decision, I would have been left in a state of real inner torment!

Then Your Excellency continued speaking in God's name: «Sister, write down the Apparitions of the Angel and of Our Lady, because, my dear Sister, this is for the glory of God and of Our Lady.»

How good God is! He is the God of peace, and it is along paths of peace that He leads those who trust in Him.

I shall begin, then, my new task, and thus fulfil the commands received from Your Excellency as well as the desires of Rev. Dr. Galamba. With the exception of that part of the Secret which I am not permitted to reveal at present, I shall say everything. I shall not knowingly omit anything, though I suppose I may forget just a few small details of minor importance.

Apparitions of the Angel

Although I cannot give the exact date, it seems to me that it was in 1915 that the first Apparition took place. As far as I can judge, it was the Angel, although at that time he did not venture to make himself fully known. From what I can recall of the weather, I think that this must have happened between the months of April and October in the year 1915.

My three companions from Casa Velha, by name Teresa Matias and her sister Maria Rosa, and Maria Justino, were with me on the southern slope of the Cabeço. We were just about to start praying the Rosary when I saw, poised in the air above the trees that stretched down to the valley which lay at our feet, what appeared to be a cloud in human form, whiter than snow and almost transparent. My companions asked me what it was. I replied that I did not know. This happened on two further occasions, but on different days.

This Apparition made a certain impression upon me, which I do not know how to explain. Little by little, this impression faded away, and were it not for the events that followed, I think I would have forgotten it completely.

The dates I cannot set down with certainty, because, at that time, I did not know how to reckon the years, the months, or even the days of the week. But I think it must have been in the spring of 1916 that the Angel appeared to us for the first time in our Loca do Cabeço.

As I have already written in my account of Jacinta, we climbed the hillside in search of shelter. After having taken our lunch and said our prayers, we began to see, some distance off, above the trees that stretched away towards the east, a light, whiter than snow, in the form of a young man, transparent, and brighter than crystal pierced by the rays of the sun. As he drew nearer, we could distinguish his features more and more clearly. We were surprised, absorbed, and struck dumb with amazement.

On reaching us, he said:

«Do not be afraid. I am the Angel of Peace. Pray with me.»

Kneeling on the ground, he bowed down until his forehead touched the earth. Led by a supernatural impulse, we did the same, and repeated the words which we heard him say:

«My God, I believe, I adore, I hope and I love You! I ask pardon of You for those who do not believe, do not adore, do not hope and do not love You!»

Having repeated these words three times, he rose and said:

«Pray thus. The Hearts of Jesus and Mary are attentive to the voice of your supplications.» Then he disappeared.

The supernatural atmosphere which enveloped us was so intense, that we were for a long time scarcely aware of our own existence, remaining in the same posture in which he had left us, and continually repeating the same prayer. The presence of God made itself felt so intimately and so intensely that we did not even venture to speak to one another. Next day, we were still immersed in this spiritual atmosphere, which only gradually began to disappear.

It did not occur to us to speak about this Apparition, nor did we think of recommending that it be kept secret. The very Apparition itself imposed secrecy. It was so intimate, that it was not easy to speak of it at all. The impression it made upon us was all the greater perhaps, in that it was the first such manifestation that we had experienced.

The second Apparition must have been at the height of summer, when the heat of the day was so intense that we had to take the sheep home before noon and only let them out again in the early evening.

We went to spend the siesta hours in the shade of the trees which surrounded the well that I have already mentioned several times. Suddenly, we saw the same Angel right beside us.

«What are you doing?» he asked. «Pray! Pray very much! The Hearts of Jesus and Mary have designs of mercy on you. Offer prayers and sacrifices constantly to the Most High.»

«How are we to make sacrifices?» I asked.

«Make of everything you can a sacrifice, and offer it to God as an act of reparation for the sins by which He is offended, and in supplication for the conversion of sinners. You will thus draw down peace upon your country. I am its Angel Guardian, the Angel of Portugal. Above all, accept and bear with submission, the suffering which the Lord will send you.»

These words were indelibly impressed upon our minds. They were like a light which made us understand who God is, how He loves us and desires to be loved, the value of sacrifice, how pleasing it is to Him and how, on account of it, He grants the grace of conversion to sinners. It was for this reason that we began, from then on, to offer to the Lord all that mortified us, without, however, seeking out other forms of mortification and penance, except that we remained for hours on end with our foreheads touching the ground, repeating the prayer the Angel had taught us.

It seems to me that the third Apparition must have been in October, or towards the end of September, as we were no longer returning home for siesta.

As I have already written in my account of Jacinta, we went one day from Pregueira (a small olive grove belonging to my parents) to the Lapa, making our way along the slope of the hill on the side facing Aljustrel and Casa Velha. We said our Rosary there and the prayer the Angel had taught us at the first Apparition.

While we were there, the Angel appeared to us for the third time, holding a chalice in his hands, with a host above it from which some drops of blood were falling into the sacred vessel. Leaving the chalice and the host suspended in the air, the Angel prostrated on the ground and repeated this prayer three times:

«Most Holy Trinity, Father, Son and Holy Spirit, I adore You profoundly, and I offer You the most precious Body, Blood, Soul and Divinity of Jesus Christ, present in all the tabernacles of the world, in reparation for the outrages, sacrileges and indifference with which He Himself is offended. And, through the infinite merits of His most Sacred Heart, and the Immaculate Heart of Mary, I beg of You the conversion of poor sinners.»

Then, rising, he once more took the chalice and the host in his hands. He gave the host to me, and to Jacinta and Francisco he gave the contents of the chalice to drink, saying as he did so: «Take and drink the Body and Blood of Jesus Christ, horribly outraged by ungrateful men. Repair their crimes and console your God.» Once again, he prostrated on the ground and repeated with us three times more, the same prayer «Most Holy Trinity...», and then disappeared.

Impelled by the power of the supernatural that enveloped us, we imitated all that the Angel had done, prostrating ourselves on the ground as he did and repeating the prayers that he said. The force of the presence of God was so intense that it absorbed us and almost completely annihilated us. It seemed to deprive us even of the use of our bodily senses for a considerable length of time. During those days, we performed all our exterior actions as though guided by that same supernatural being who was impelling us thereto. The peace and happiness which we felt were great, but wholly interior, for our souls were completely immersed in God. The physical exhaustion that came over us was also great.

Lucia's Silence

I do not know why, but the Apparitions of Our Lady produced in us very different effects. We felt the same intimate joy, the same peace and happiness, but instead of physical prostration, an expansive ease of movement; instead of this annihilation in the Divine Presence, a joyful exultation; instead of the difficulty in speaking, we felt a certain communicative enthusiasm. Despite these feelings, however, we felt inspired to be silent, especially concerning certain things.

Whenever I was interrogated, I experienced an interior inspiration which directed me how to answer, without either failing in truth or revealing what should remain hidden for the time being. In this respect, I still have just this one doubt: «Should I not have said everything in the canonical enquiry?» But I have no scruples about having kept silence, because at that time I had as yet no realization of the importance of this particular interrogation. I regarded it, at the time, as being just like the many other interrogations to which I was accustomed. The only thing I thought strange was the order to take the oath. But as it was my confessor who told me to do so, and as I was swearing to the truth, I took the oath without any difficulty. Little did I suspect, at that moment, that the devil would make the most of this, in order to torment me with endless scruples later on. But, thank God, all that is over now.

There was yet another reason which confirmed me in my conviction that I did well to remain silent. In the course of the canonical enquiry, one of the interrogators, Rev. Dr. Marques dos Santos, thought he could extend somewhat his questionnaire, and began therefore to ask more searching questions. Before answering, I looked enquiringly at my confessor. His Reverence saved me from my predicament, and answered on my behalf. He reminded the interrogator that he was exceeding his rights in this matter.

Almost the same thing happened when I was questioned by Rev. Dr. Fischer. He had the authorization of Your Excellency and of Rev. Mother Provincial, and seemed to have the right to question me on everything. But, thank God, he came accompanied by my confessor. At a given moment, he put to me a carefully studied question about the Secret. I felt perplexed, and did not know how to answer. I glanced towards my confessor; he understood me and answered for me. The interrogator understood also, and confined himself to picking up some magazines lying nearby and holding them in front of my face. In this way, God was showing me that the moment appointed by Him had not yet arrived.

I shall now go on to write about the Apparitions of Our Lady. I shall not delay over the circumstances that preceded or followed them, since Rev. Dr. Galamba has kindly dispensed me from doing so.

The 13th of May, 1917

High up on the slope in the Cova da Iria, I was playing with Jacinta and Francisco at building a little stone wall around a clump of furze. Suddenly we saw what seemed to be a flash of lightning.

«We'd better go home,» I said to my cousins, «that's lightning; we may have a thunderstorm.»

«Yes, indeed!» they answered.

We began to go down the slope, hurrying the sheep along towards the road. We were more or less half-way down the slope, and almost level with a large holmoak tree that stood there, when we saw another flash of lightning. We had only gone a few steps further when, there before us on a small holmoak, we beheld a Lady all dressed in white. She was more brilliant than the sun, and radiated a light more clear and intense than a crystal glass filled with sparkling water, when the rays of the burning sun shine through it.

We stopped, astounded, before the Apparition. We were so close, just a few feet from her, that we were bathed in the light which surrounded her, or rather, which radiated from her. Then Our Lady spoke to us:

«Do not be afraid. I will do you no harm.»

«Where are you from?»

«I am from heaven.»

«What do you want of me?»

«I have come to ask you to come here for six months in succession, on the 13th day, at this same hour. Later on, I will tell you who I am and what I want. Afterwards, I will return here yet a seventh time.» [12]

«Shall I go to heaven too?»

perplexa sem saber que responder. Um olhar! o confessor tinha-me entendido e respondia por mim: o interrogante entendeu também, e limitou-se a tapar-me a cara com umas devistas que tinha diante.

Assim Deus, me ia mostrando que ainda não era chegado o momento por Êle designado.

Para então a escrever as aparições de nossa senhora, não me detenho a escrever as circumstâncias que as precederam, nem as que se lhe seguiram, visto o senhor Dr. Galamba ter feito o favor de me dispensar d'isso.

Dia 13 de Maio 1917.— Andando a brincar com a Jacinta e o Francisco, no cimo da encosta da Cova de Iria, a fazer uma paredita em volta d'uma moita, vimos derrepente como que um relampago. É melhor irmos embora para casa, disse a meus primos: que estão a fazer relampagos, pode vir trovoada. Pois sim. E começamos a descer a encosta, tocando as ovelhas em direcção à estrada. Ao chegar, mais ou menos a meio da encosta, quasi se junto d'uma azinheira grande que ai havia vimos então relampago, e dado alguns passos

«Yes, you will.»

«And Jacinta?»

«She will go also.»

«And Francisco?»

«He will go there too, but he must say many Rosaries.»

Then I remembered to ask about two girls who had died recently. They were friends of mine and used to come to my home to learn weaving with my eldest sister.

«Is Maria das Neves in heaven?»

«Yes, she is.» (I think she was about 16 years old).

«And Amélia?»

«She will be in purgatory until the end of the world.» [13] (It seems to me that she was between 18 and 20 years of age).

«Are you willing to offer yourselves to God and bear all the sufferings He wills to send you, as an act of reparation for the sins by which He is offended, and of supplication for the conversion of sinners?»

«Yes, we are willing.»

«Then you are going to have much to suffer, but the grace of God will be your comfort.»

As she pronounced these last words «...the grace of God will be your comfort», Our Lady opened her hands for the first time, communicating to us a light so intense that, as it streamed from her hands, its rays penetrated our hearts and the innermost depths of our souls, making us see ourselves in God, Who was that light, more clearly than we see ourselves in the best of mirrors. Then, moved by an interior impulse that was also communicated to us, we fell on our knees, repeating in our hearts:

«O most Holy Trinity, I adore You! My God, my God, I love You in the most Blessed Sacrament!»

After a few moments, Our Lady spoke again:

«Pray the Rosary every day, in order to obtain peace for the world, and the end of the war.»

Then she began to rise serenely, going up towards the east, until she disappeared in the immensity of space. The light that surrounded her seemed to open up a path before her in the firmament, and for this reason we sometimes said that we saw heaven opening.

I think that I have already explained in my account of Jacinta, or else in a letter, that the fear which we felt was not really fear of Our Lady, but rather fear of the thunderstorm

mais adiante vimos sôbre uma carrasqueira, uma senhora, vestida tôda de branco, mais brilhante que o sol, espargindo-luz, mais clara e intensa que um copo de cristal, cheio d'água cristalina atravessado pelos raios do sol. Mais ardente. ficamos surprehendidos, pela aparição. Estávamos tam perto que ficávamos dentro-da luz que a cercava. ou que Ela espargia-, talvez a metro e meio de distância mais ou menos.

Então nossa senhora disse-nos; não tenhais medo, eu não vos faço mal. De donde é vossemecê? lhe preguntei. sou do Céu. E que é que vossemecê me quer? Vim para vos pedir que venhais aqui seis mezes seguidos, no dia 13 a esta mesma hora, depois vos direi quem sou e o que quero. Depois voltarei ainda aqui uma setima-vez. E eu, também vou para o Céu? Sim, vais. E a Jacinta? Também. E o Francisco? Também, mas tem que rezar muitos terços.

lembrei-me então de preguntar por duas rapariguas que tinham morrido á pouco, eram minhas amigas e estavam em minha-casa a aprender a teceiras com minha Irmã mais velha.

which we thought was coming, and it was from this that we sought to escape. The Apparitions of Our Lady inspired neither fear nor fright, but rather surprise. When I was asked if I had experienced fear, and I said that we had, I was referring to the fear we felt when we saw the flashes of lightning and thought that a thunderstorm was at hand. It was from this that we wished to escape, as we were used to seeing lightning only when it thundered. Besides, the flashes of lightning were not really lightning, but the reflected rays of a light which was approaching. It was because we saw the light, that we sometimes said we saw Our Lady coming; but, properly speaking, we only perceived Our Lady in that light when she was already on the holmoak tree. The fact that we did not know how to explain this, and that we wished to avoid questions, caused us to say sometimes that we saw her coming, and other times that we did not. When we said we saw her coming, we were referring to the approach of the light, which after all was herself. And when we said we did not see her coming, we were referring to the fact that we really saw Our Lady only when she was on the holmoak.

The 13th of June, 1917

As soon as Jacinta, Francisco and I had finished praying the Rosary, with a number of other people who were present, we saw once more the flash reflecting the light which was approaching (which we called lightning). The next moment, Our Lady was there on the holmoak, exactly the same as in May.

«What do you want of me?» I asked.

«I wish you to come here on the 13th of next month, to pray the Rosary every day, and to learn to read. Later, I will tell you what I want.»

I asked for the cure of a sick person.

«If he is converted, he will be cured during the year.»

«I would like to ask you to take us to heaven.»

«Yes. I will take Jacinta and Francisco soon. But you are to stay here some time longer. Jesus wishes to make use of you to make me known and loved. He wants to establish in the world devotion to my Immaculate Heart.» [14]

«Am I to stay here alone?» I asked, sadly.

«No, my daughter. Are you suffering a great deal? Don't lose heart. I will never forsake you. My Immaculate Heart

reparação.

Eis Exmo. e Rvmo. Senhor Bispo ao que
nos referiamos quando diziamos que Nossa Senho-
.a nos tinha revelado um segredo em junho.
Nossa Senhora não nos mandou ainda d'esta vez
guardar segredo, mas sentiamos isso que Deus a
isso nos movia.

Dia 13 de Julho de 1917. momentos depois
de termos chegado á Cova de Iria, junto da
carrasqueira, entre immensa multidão de
povo, estando a rezar o terço, vimos o reflexo
da costumada luz e em seguida Nossa Senhora
sôbre a carrasqueira.

Vossemecê que me quer? (perguntei) Quero
que venham aqui no dia 13 do mez que vem, que
continuem a rezar o terço todos os dias, em
honra de Nossa Senhora do Rosário para obter
a paz do mundo e o fim da guerra, porque só
ela lhes poderá valer.

Quero pedir-lhe para nos dizer quem é,
para fazer um milagre com que todos acredi-
tem que Vossemecê nos apparece.

will be your refuge and the way that will lead you to God.»

As Our Lady spoke these last words, she opened her hands and for the second time, she communicated to us the rays of that same immense light. We saw ourselves in this light, as it were, immersed in God. Jacinta and Francisco seemed to be in that part of the light which rose towards heaven, and I in that which was poured out on the earth. In front of the palm of Our Lady's right hand was a heart encircled by thorns which pierced it. We understood that this was the Immaculate Heart of Mary, outraged by the sins of humanity, and seeking reparation.

You know now, Your Excellency, what we referred to when we said that Our Lady had revealed a secret to us in June. At the time, Our Lady did not tell us to keep it secret, but we felt moved to do so by God.

The 13th of July, 1917

A few moments after arriving at the Cova da Iria, near the holmoak, where a large number of people were praying the Rosary, we saw the flash of light once more, and a moment later Our Lady appeared on the holmoak.

«What do you want of me?» I asked.

«I want you to come here on the 13th of next month, to continue to pray the Rosary every day in honour of Our Lady of the Rosary, in order to obtain peace for the world and the end of the war, because only she can help you.»

«I would like to ask you to tell us who you are, and to work a miracle so that everybody will believe that you are appearing to us.»

«Continue to come here every month. In October, I will tell you who I am and what I want, and I will perform a miracle for all to see and believe.»

I then made some requests, but I cannot recall now just what they were. What I do remember is that Our Lady said it was necessary for such people to pray the Rosary in order to obtain these graces during the year. And she continued:

«Sacrifice yourselves for sinners, and say many times, especially whenever you make some sacrifice: O Jesus, it is for love of You, for the conversion of sinners, and in reparation for the sins committed against the Immaculate Heart of Mary.»

As Our Lady spoke these last words, she opened her

73

Continuem a vir aqui todos os mezes, em Outubro direi quem sou, o que quero e farei um milagre que todos andem ver para acreditar.

Aqui fiz alguns pedidos que não recordo bem quais foram. O que me lembro é que, Nossa Senhora disse que era preciso rezarem o terço para alcançarem as graças durante o ano. E continuou. Sacrificai-vos pelos pecadores, e dizei muitas vezes, em especial, sempre que fizerdes algum sacrifício. Ó Jesus é por vosso amor, pela conversão dos pecadores e em reparação pelos pecados cometidos contra o Imaculado Coração de Maria.

Ao dizer estas últimas palavras abriu de novo as mãos como nos dois mezes passados.

O reflexo parece penetra-a terra e vimos como que um mar de fogo, mergulhados em êsse fogo os demonios e as almas, como se fossem brazas transparentes e negras ou bronzeadas com forma humana, que flutuavam no incen- dio, levadas pelas chamas que d'elas mesmas saíam juntamente com nuvens de fumo, caindo para todos os lados semelhante ao

hands once more, as she had done during the two previous months. The rays of light seemed to penetrate the earth, and we saw as it were a sea of fire. Plunged in this fire were demons and souls in human form, like transparent burning embers, all blackened or burnished bronze, floating about in the conflagration, now raised into the air by the flames that issued from within themselves together with great clouds of smoke, now falling back on every side like sparks in huge fires, without weight or equilibrium, amid shrieks and groans of pain and despair, which horrified us and made us tremble with fear. (It must have been this sight which caused me to cry out, as people say they heard me). The demons could be distinguished by their terrifying and repellent likeness to frightful and unknown animals, black and transparent like burning coals. Terrified and as if to plead for succour, we looked up at Our Lady, who said to us, so kindly and so sadly:

«You have seen hell where the souls of poor sinners go. To save them, God wishes to establish in the world devotion to my Immaculate Heart. If what I say to you is done, many souls will be saved and there will be peace. The war is going to end; but if people do not cease offending God, a worse one will break out during the pontificate of Pius XI. When you see a night illumined by an unknown light, [15] know that this is the great sign given you by God that he is about to punish the world for its crimes, by means of war, famine, and persecutions of the Church and of the Holy Father.

«To prevent this, I shall come to ask for the consecration of Russia to my Immaculate Heart, and the Communion of Reparation on the First Saturdays. [16] If my requests are heeded, Russia will be converted, and there will be peace; [17] if not, she will spread her errors throughout the world, causing wars and persecutions of the Church. The good will be martyred, the Holy Father will have much to suffer, various nations will be annihilated. In the end, my Immaculate Heart will triumph. The Holy Father will consecrate Russia to me, and she will be converted, and a period of peace will be granted to the world. In Portugal, the dogma of the Faith will always be preserved; etc... Do not tell this to anybody. Francisco, yes, you may tell him.

«When you pray the Rosary, say after each mystery: O my Jesus, forgive us, save us from the fire of hell. Lead

caír das faulhas em os grandes, num pro
nem iquilibrio entre gritos e gemidos de dôr
e dispero que horrorizava e fazia estreme-
cer de pavor. (devem ser ao reparar-me com esta
vista que dei êsse ai, que dizem terme ouvido). Os
demónios destinguiam-se por fórmas horriveis
e asserosas de animais espantosos e desconhecidos,
mas transparentes como negros carvões em
braza. Assustados e como que a pedir soccor-
ro levantamos a vista para Nossa Senhora
que nos disse com bondade e tristeza. Vistês
o inferno, para onde vão as almas dos pobres
pecadores; para as salvar Deus quer estabeleer
no mundo a devoção a meu Imaculado
Coração, se fizerem o que eu vos disser salvar-
se-ão muitas almas e terão paz: a guerra
vai acabar: mas se não deixarem de ofender a
Deus, no reinado de Pio XI começará outra
peor. Quando virdes uma noite alumeada por
uma luz desconhecida, sabei que é o grande
sinal que Deus vos dá deque vai a punir o
mundo de seus crimes, por meio da guerra, da
fome e de perseguições à Igreja e ao Santo Padre.

all souls to heaven, especially those who are most in need.»

After this, there was a moment of silence, and then I asked:

«Is there anything more that you want of me?»

«No, I do not want anything more of you today.»

Then, as before Our Lady began to ascend towards the east, until she finally disappeared in the immense distance of the firmament.

The 13th of August, 1917

As I have already said what happened on this day, I will not delay over it here, but pass on to the Apparition which, in my opinion, took place on the 15th in the afternoon. [18] As at that time I did not yet know how to reckon the days of the month, it could be that I am mistaken. But I still have an idea that it took place on the very day that we arrived back from Vila Nova de Ourém.

I was accompanied by Francisco and his brother John. We were with the sheep in a place called Valinhos, when we felt something supernatural approaching and enveloping us. Suspecting that Our Lady was about to appear to us, and feeling sorry lest Jacinta might miss seeing her, we asked her brother to go and call her. As he was unwilling to go, I offered him two small coins, and off he ran.

Meanwhile, Francisco and I saw the flash of light, which we called lightning. Jacinta arrived, and a moment later, we saw Our Lady on a holmoak tree.

«What do you want of me?»

«I want you to continue going to the Cova da Iria on the 13th, and to continue praying the Rosary every day. In the last month, I will perform a miracle so that all may believe.»

«What do you want done with the money that the people leave in the Cova da Iria?»

«Have two litters made. One is to be carried by you and Jacinta and two other girls dressed in white; the other one is to be carried by Francisco and three other boys. The money from the litters is for the «festa» of Our Lady of the Rosary, and what is left over will help towards the construction of a chapel that is to be built here.»

«I would like to ask you to cure some sick persons.»

75

Para a conseguir, virei pedir a consagração da Russia a meu Imaculado Coração, e a comunhão reparadora nos primeiros sábados. Se atenderem a meus pedidos a Russia se converterá e terão paz: se não, espalhará seus erros pelo mundo, promovendo guerras e perseguições à Igreja, os bons serão martirizados, e santo Padre terá muito que sofrer, varias nações serão aniquiladas: por fim o meu Imaculado Coração triunfará. O santo Padre consagrar-me-á a Russia que se converterá e será concedido ao mundo algum tempo de paz. Em Portugal se conservará sempre o dogma da fé etc. Isto não o digais a ninguem. a Francisco sim, podeis dize-lo.

Quando rezais o terço, dizei depois de cada misterio. O meu Jesus perdoai-nos, livrai-nos do fogo do inferno, levai as alminhas todas para o céu, principalmente aquelas que mais precisarem. Seguiu-se um instante de silencio e perguntei. Vossemecê, não me quer mais nada? não, hoje não te quero mais nada. E como de costume começou a elevar-se em direção ao nascente.

«Yes, I will cure some of them during the year.»

Then, looking very sad, Our Lady said:

«Pray, pray very much, and make sacrifices for sinners; for many souls go to hell, because there are none to sacrifice themselves and to pray for them.»

And she began to ascend as usual towards the east.

The 13th of September, 1917

As the hour approached, I set out with Jacinta and Francisco, but owing to the crowds around us we could only advance with difficulty. The roads were packed with people, and everyone wanted to see us and speak to us. There was no human respect whatsoever. Simple folk, and even ladies and gentlemen, struggled to break through the crowd that pressed around us. No sooner had they reached us than they threw themselves on their knees before us, begging us to place their petitions before Our Lady. Others who could not get close to us shouted from a distance:

«For the love of God, ask Our Lady to cure my son who is a cripple!» Yet another cried out: «And to cure mine who is blind!... To cure mine who is deaf!... To bring back my husband, my son, who has gone to the war!... To convert a sinner!... To give me back my health as I have tuberculosis!» and so on.

All the afflictions of poor humanity were assembled there. Some climbed up to the tops of trees and walls to see us go by, and shouted down to us. Saying yes to some, giving a hand to others and helping them up from the dusty ground, we managed to move forward, thanks to some gentlemen who went ahead and opened a passage for us through the multitude.

Now, when I read in the New Testament about those enchanting scenes of Our Lord's passing through Palestine, I think of those which Our Lord allowed me to witness, while yet a child, on the poor roads and lanes from Aljustrel to Fatima and on to the Cova da Iria! I give thanks to God, offering Him the faith of our good Portuguese people, and I think: «If these people so humbled themselves before three poor children, just because they were mercifully granted the grace to speak to the Mother of God, what would they not do if they saw Our Lord Himself in person before them?»

Well, none of this was called for here! It was a distraction of my pen, leading me away where I did not mean to go. But, never mind! It's just another useless digression. I am not tearing it out, so as not to spoil the notebook.

At last, we arrived at the Cova da Iria, and on reaching the holmoak we began to say the Rosary with the people. Shortly afterwards, we saw the flash of light, and then Our Lady appeared on the holmoak.

«Continue to pray the Rosary in order to obtain the end of the war. In October Our Lord will come, as well as Our Lady of Dolours and Our Lady of Carmel. Saint Joseph will appear with the Child Jesus to bless the world. God is pleased with your sacrifices. He does not want you to sleep with the rope on, but only to wear it during the daytime.»

«I was told to ask you many things, the cure of some sick people, of a deaf-mute...»

«Yes, I will cure some, but not others. In October I will perform a miracle so that all may believe.»

Then Our Lady began to rise as usual, and disappeared.

The 13th of October, 1917

We left home quite early, expecting that we would be delayed along the way. Masses of people thronged the roads. The rain fell in torrents. My mother, her heart torn with uncertainty as to what was going to happen, and fearing it would be the last day of my life, wanted to accompany me.

On the way, the scenes of the previous month, still more numerous and moving, were repeated. Not even the muddy roads could prevent these people from kneeling in the most humble and suppliant of attitudes. We reached the holmoak in the Cova da Iria. Once there, moved by an interior impulse, I asked the people to shut their umbrellas and say the Rosary. A little later, we saw the flash of light, and then Our Lady appeared on the holmoak.

«What do you want of me?»

«I want to tell you that a chapel is to be built here in my honour. I am the Lady of the Rosary. Continue always to pray the Rosary every day. The war is going to end, and the soldiers will soon return to their homes.»

«I have many things to ask you: the cure of some sick persons, the conversion of sinners, and other things...»

«Some yes, but not others. They must amend their lives and ask forgiveness for their sins.»

172

Looking very sad, Our Lady said:

«Do not offend the Lord our God any more, because He is already so much offended.»

Then, opening her hands, she made them reflect on the sun, and as she ascended, the reflection of her own light continued to be projected on the sun itself.

Here, Your Excellency, is the reason why I cried out to the people to look at the sun. My aim was not to call their attention to the sun, because I was not even aware of their presence. I was moved to do so under the guidance of an interior impulse.

After Our Lady had disappeared into the immense distance of the firmament, we beheld St. Joseph with the Child Jesus and Our Lady robed in white with a blue mantle, beside the sun. St. Joseph and the Child Jesus appeared to bless the world, for they traced the Sign of the Cross with their hands. When, a little later, this apparition disappeared, I saw Our Lord and Our Lady; it seemed to me that it was Our Lady of Dolours. Our Lord appeared to bless the world in the same manner as St. Joseph had done. This apparition also vanished, and I saw Our Lady once more, this time resembling Our Lady of Carmel.

EPILOGUE

Here then, Your Excellency, you have the story of the Apparitions of Our Lady in the Cova da Iria, in 1917. Whenever and for whatever motive I had to speak of them, I sought to do so in as few words as possible, with the desire of keeping to myself alone those more intimate aspects which were so difficult for me to reveal. But as they belong to God and not to me, and as He now, through Your Excellency, requires them of me, here they are. I return what does not belong to me. To the best of my knowledge, I keep nothing back. I think I have only omitted some minor details referring to the petitions which I made. As these were merely material things, I did not attach such great importance to them, and it is perhaps because of this that they did not make such a vivid impression on my mind; and then there were so many of them, so very many! It was possibly because I was so anxious to remember the innumerable graces that I had to ask of Our Lady, that I was mistaken when I understood that the war would end on that very 13th. [19]

Not a few people have expressed considerable surprise at the memory that God has deigned to give me. In this matter indeed I have, through His infinite goodness, been quite favoured in every respect. Where supernatural things are concerned, this is not to be wondered at, for these are imprinted on the mind in such a way that it is almost impossible to forget them. At least, the meaning of what is made known is never forgotten, unless it be that God also wills that this too be forgotten.

111. FURTHER RECOLLECTIONS OF JACINTA

A Wonderful Cure

Furthermore, Rev. Dr. Galamba has asked me to write down any other favour that may have been obtained by means of Jacinta. I have given the matter some thought and can recall only two instances.

I spoke of Senhora Emilia in the second account of Jacinta. The first time that this kind lady came to take me to the priest's house in Olival, Jacinta went there with me. When we reached the village where that good widow lived, it was already night. In spite of this, news of our arrival quickly spread abroad, and Senhora Emilia's house was soon surrounded by a crowd of people. They all wanted to see us, question us, ask for graces, and so on.

It happened that a certain devout woman from a little village nearby was accustomed to recite the Rosary in her own home, in company with any of the neighbours who wished to join her. She, therefore, invited us to go and pray the Rosary in her house. We sought to excuse ourselves, explaining that we were going to say it with Senhora Emilia, but she spoke so insistently that there was nothing to do but to yield to her request. When the news went round that we were going there, crowds of people hurried to the good woman's house in the hope of securing a good place. This was all the better for us, since we found the road comparatively free.

On our way to the house, a girl about twenty years old came out to meet us. Weeping, she knelt down, and begged us to enter her house and say at least one Hail Mary for the recovery of her father, who for three years had been unable to take any rest, on account of continual hiccoughs. In such circumstances, it was impossible to resist. I helped the poor girl to her feet. As it was already late into the night, and we were finding our way along by the light of lanterns, I therefore told Jacinta to remain there, while I went on ahead to pray the Rosary with the people, promising to call for her on my return. She agreed. When I came back I, too, went into the house. I found Jacinta sitting on a chair, facing a man who was also seated. He was not so very old but he looked emaciated, and he was weeping with emotion. Some persons were gathered around him, members of his family, I should think. On seeing me Jacinta got up, said goodbye and promised that she would not forget him in her prayers. Then we returned to Senhora Emilia's house.

Early next morning, we set out for Olival, and only came back three days later. When we reached Senhora Emilia's house, there we found the happy girl accompanied by her father. He now looked much better, and had lost all trace of nervous strain and extreme weakness. They came to thank us for the grace they had received for, they said, he was no longer troubled by the annoying hiccoughs.

The Prodigal Son

The other favour was received by an aunt of mine called Vitoria, who was married and lived in Fatima. She had a son who was a real prodigal. I do not know the reason, but he left his father's house, and no one knew what had become of him. In her distress, my aunt came to Aljustrel one day to ask me to pray to Our Lady for this son of hers. Not finding me, she asked Jacinta instead, who promised to pray for him. A few days later, he suddenly returned home, asked his parents' forgiveness, and then went to Aljustrel to relate his sorry story.

He told us that, after having spent all that he had stolen from his parents, he wandered about for quite a while like a tramp until, for some reason I have now forgotten, he was put in jail at Torres Novas. After he had been there for some time, he succeeded in escaping one night and fled to the remote hills and unfamiliar pine groves. Realizing he had completely lost his way, and torn between the fear of being captured and the darkness of a stormy night, he found that his only recourse was prayer. Falling on his knees, he began to pray. Some minutes had passed, he affirmed, when Jacinta appeared to him, took him by the hand and led him to the main road which runs from Alqueidão to Reguengo, making a sign for him to continue in that direction. When morning dawned, he found himself on the road to Boleiros. Recognizing the place where he was, he was overcome with emotion and directed his steps straight home to his parents.

Now what he declared was that Jacinta had appeared to him, and that he had recognized her perfectly. I asked Jacinta if it was true that she had gone there to guide him. She answered that she had not, that she had no idea at all of the location of the pine woods and hills where he had been lost.

«I only prayed and pleaded very much with Our Lady for him, because I felt so sorry for Aunt Vitoria.» That was how she answered me.

How, then, did it happen? I don't know. Only God knows.

IV. **NOTES ON FR. FONSECA'S BOOK**

PROLOGUE

Now, Your Excellency, it is time to comment on the book «Our Lady of Fatima» by Rev. Fr. Luís Gonzaga Aires de Fonseca, S. J. [20]

Rev. Dr. Galamba told me to make a note of anything which I found in the book that was not quite exact. I have only found a few small details, which are hardly worth mentioning. But as there is question of his writing another book, and as Your Excellency so desires it, I shall note these things down to prevent their being repeated.

Annotations

In Chapter 11, page 18, it says: «A small piece of uncultivated ground». Wholly uncultivated, no. In the Cova we grew maize, potatoes, beans, wheat, etc. — whatever was being sown at the time. On the slopes, especially the one leading towards the roadway, there grew some holmoaks and olive trees, which produced acorns and olives.

Chapter 11, page 19, states: «They looked towards the right, etc.» No. In such a case, it would be towards the left, or straight ahead. The slope which goes up to the spot where we happened to be playing, was criss-crossed by numerous tracks and furrows, leaving only one pathway. On the extreme left on the way up, these tracks were formed by rows of holmoaks, both large and small, all growing at random, and which together with the furze bushes formed dense thickets, making it difficult to get through. Taking the pathway on the right side going down, we went towards the large holmoak tree, and thus the small one was well to the left of us.

A little further back, in the same paragraph, it is stated that the second flash rooted us to the spot where we were. This also is inexact. We saw it when we were halfway down the slope which runs from the place of the Apparitions to the top of the hill, just before we reached the big holmoak. [21] We kept on going until we came face to face with Our Lady on the small holmoak.

On the same page 19, it also says: «Amazed, they wished to flee.» This is also incorrect. I think I have already explained this in another account. As soon as we saw Our Lady, we never gave another thought to running away. Our Lady does not cause fear, but only surprise, peace and joy.

When we said we had been afraid, we were referring to the fear we felt at the thought of a coming thunderstorm, and that was why we wanted to run. I think that when Our Lady told us not to be afraid, she wanted to calm our fears of the thunderstorm that we supposed was coming, for we were used to seeing lightning only when there was a storm. In our ignorance, we were as yet unable to distinguish between the flash of light and the lightning.

Chapter 11, page 20, says: «Almost the same length as the dress». I think this «almost» should be eliminated, because it was of the same length.

In the same Chapter 11, page 21, it says: «What have you come to do here?» I do not remember asking that question.

Chapter 111, page 29, states: «She then confided a secret to them, and strictly forbade them to reveal it.» As I have already said above in my account of the Apparitions, in this particular month it was we ourselves who wished to keep the light and its effects secret. It was in the following month that the Secret was imposed on us by Our Lady.

In the account of the Apparitions which the writer gives

here, there are some small details that it seems to me quite useless to point out, since I have already written everything exactly as it happened. Furthermore, some of these details spring from the manner of expression used by the writer.

Chapter V, page 45, says: «Crying from fear». Jacinta wept in prison because she missed her mother and her family; but she did not cry during the interrogation.

Chapter V, page 46, says: «The boy followed him, crying». He did not cry.

Chapter V, page 47, states: «They went, running, to the Cova da Iria.» We only went to the Cova da Iria after the Apparition in Valinhos, some days later.

Chapter VII, page 60, says: «The dress has gold lines». It had no lines at all. When Francisco said that, he was perhaps referring to the undulating effect of the light surrounding the dress.

Chapter VII, page 64, says: «Small earrings». I didn't see any earrings. I remember a golden cord which, like a brilliant sunbeam, seemed to border her mantle. It was reflected in the space left by the mantle as it fell from the head to the shoulders, shimmering in the light which enveloped Our Lady's whole person in undulating variations, which momentarily gave the impression of small earrings. I must have been referring to this when I gave that reply.

Chapter VII, page 66, gives these words: «Could you not at least tell it to your confessor? She seemed somewhat puzzled, and remained silent.» I was perplexed and did not know how to reply, because I kept several things secret which I was not forbidden to reveal. But I thank God who inspired my questioner to go on with the interrogation. I remember how I breathed again.

Chapter VII, page 73, says: «Is this how you fulfil the order that Our Lady gave you.» I kept silence, not wishing to put the blame on my mother, who at that time had not yet allowed me to go to school. At home, they said it was out of vanity that I wanted to learn to read. Until then, hardly any girls learned to read. The school was just for boys. It was only later that a school was opened in Fatima for girls.

INTERROGATION BY THE AUTHOR
ANTERO DE FIGUEIREDO

Chapter XIII, page 158, states in the note: «Rev. Mother Monfalim was present at all the author's interviews with Sister Dores.» This is not true. Only Dr. Antero de Figueiredo's daughter, who accompanied him, was present. Mother Monfalim, who was then my Provincial Superior, was in Tuy. From there, she wrote me a letter which she sent, unsealed, by Dr. Antero de Figueiredo to Pontevedra, where I then was. There the interrogation took place, and it was one of the most difficult interrogations that God has made me undergo. [22]

In this letter, Rev. Mother Provincial ordered me to answer, with sincerity, truthfulness and simplicity, everything that Dr. Antero de Figueiredo wished to ask me. She requested that I offer to God this act of obedience.

Before handing me the letter, he read it. The order given me, that under obedience I was to answer everything with sincerity, pleased him; he judged that he could, therefore, put to me any question whatsoever that his mind might devise. As if that were not enough, he had his daughter's head beside him, ready to conjure up more questions.

For my part, I was not slow in realizing how far he intended to go with his interrogation. I asked myself if I would now have to reveal my most intimate secrets, those which I had so far kept with such great care, and reveal them moreover to a lay man, who seemed to me not only to know nothing about the spiritual life, but not even to understand the bare essentials of the practice of the christian life. To avoid making rash judgements and in order to be sure as to how things stood, I tried to phrase my answers precisely in such a way as to draw from him an admission of the truth. In fact, he was deeply moved, and confessed more than once, with tears streaming down his cheeks, the black spots of his sorry life. Afterwards, I regretted having given occasion for such sad avowals, but it was then too late. In spite of begging him not to make known to me such things, of which I knew little or nothing, his emotional state was such that he could not refrain from doing so, and I had to resign myself to listening to it all.

Meanwhile, I was thinking: «Have I to manifest my intimate secrets to this man? Impossible! And what about obedience? I don't know!» The local Mother Superior had received orders to be present at the interrogation. But, not wanting such a responsibility, she had excused herself owing to lack of time, and had withdrawn. I then asked to leave the room for a moment, and I went to place my doubts before her and ask her advice. Mother Superior replied that, in view of Mother Provincial's order, she did not know how to advise me. I then asked to speak to the confessor, but he was absent, and nobody knew when he was due to return. I went to the chapel. I offered a brief prayer to Jesus in the Blessed Sacrament and to Our Lady, and then returned to the parlour once more. The interrogation began again, and it was of such a kind as to draw out of me all that I kept locked within my heart. But the repugnance I felt at the thought of revealing it only increased, and the struggle between this and the doubt as to whether or not obedience obliged me to reveal it grew stronger and stronger. I soon discovered that the good man sought to study me in depth.

The first and second day over, we reached the third day of the interrogation, and I became more and more perplexed. On the afternoon of the third day, it seemed that God willed to grant me a ray of His light. From the parlour I heard a voice in the hallway, that of a Jesuit priest whom I had known in Tuy, Rev. Dr. Herrera. Without loss of time, I asked to leave the room for a moment, and made my way to Mother Superior to ask permission to speak to him. Right then, I wanted nothing further from His Reverence than that he would tell me how far obedience obliged me to manifest myself. But God wanted sacrifice! Did He not also find Himself alone in the Garden of Olives? And is He not still alone in so many abandoned tabernacles? We must keep Him company and remain at His side, not only in the breaking of the bread, but also in the drinking of the chalice.

It was certainly through this dispensation of the Almighty that Rev. Mother Superior refused me permission to speak to the venerable Jesuit priest. With a heart even heavier than when I left, I went back to the parlour. The interrogation continued, becoming more and more detailed every moment. The fourth day came, still darker than the three preceding ones. There was already considerable discontent in the community. A lot of work needed to be done in the house, and there was I doing nothing! As far as they could see, I was having a fine time in the parlour, and therefore making no attempt to bring the visit to a speedy conclusion. Mother Superior was already showing how displeased she was, also. Had they been able to read my heart, O my God, they would have seen how greatly I would have preferred, had I been given the choice, a brush with which to scrub the house rather than the padded chair on which they saw me so comfortably seated! But we must not let the breath of creatures dull the mirror that shines brightly in the sight of God. And then, I must confess, were it not for the word «Obedience» that Mother Provincial put in her letter, the interrogator would have had to return home on the very first day with his list of questions just the same as he had brought it, as indeed had happened to him the previous year.

«What am I to do?» I asked myself, without being able to arrive at any decision. The interrogation seemed to be still very far from coming to an end. God be thanked, I found that a trustworthy messenger was going straight to Tuy that very afternoon. I hastily wrote down on a sheet of paper the main difficulties facing me and sent it to Rev. Mother Provincial, begging the favour of an urgent reply by telephone. The following morning at nine o'clock, Mother Lemos, the Mistress of Novices, gave the answer over the phone on behalf of Mother Provincial.

«You can keep silent,» she said, «about everything you do not wish to make known. Do not send the interrogator away, but rather give a satisfactory answer to all his questions, however long the interrogation might last.»

Good! On the strength of this reply, I began the fifth day, with my spirit no longer clouded over. Why worry about the external conflicts instigated by the devil, as long as I had in my soul the inner certainty that I was fulfilling God's will, as made known to me through obedience? The interrogation continued for several days more. At its close, I followed the advice of our confessor, who had just returned that very day, and firmly told the interrogator that he was absolutely forbidden to publish or make known anything whatsoever of all that I had told him, without the express approbation of Your Excellency and of Rev. Mother Provincial. The good gentleman was by no means pleased with such a proposition, and did everything he could to persuade me to revoke it. I saw that I would be obliged to take a firm stand. Strengthened, however, by the divine Holy Spirit, I stood firm right to the end.

You know now, Your Excellency, what happened during Dr. Antero de Figueiredo's interrogation. As you can see, this was the time I felt most keenly that God alone was with me.

During the interrogation, there was yet another doubt that tormented me, and that was the absence of any authorization on the part of Your Excellency. I asked myself: «Did Rev. Mother Provincial ask the Bishop's permission before she gave me this order? Would His Excellency be happy to have me subjected to such an interrogation without his authorization? And what about the order His Excellency gave me that I am not to speak about these things?» It was because of all these doubts that I wrote a full account of the whole affair to Your Excellency. The good Lord was pleased to permit that I received no answer to my letter, and I therefore left the whole matter in God's hands.

Final Annotations

Chapter VII, page 77, reads as follows: «The little shepherds arrived, rather better dressed than usual. The little girls wore sky blue dresses, with white veils and wreaths of flowers on their heads, etc.» I think that this is incorrect. I seem to recall that a lady did indeed appear and she wished to dress us up like that, but we refused. What I do remember well about that particular day is that I arrived home without my plaits, which I wore down to my waist, and that my mother was most upset when she saw that I had even less hair than Francisco. Who stole my plaits? I don't know. Amid the crush of such a multitude, there was no lack of scissors or thieving hands. It was easy enough to lose my kerchief, even if in fact it wasn't stolen. Already, in the two previous months, quite a lot of my plaits had been snipped off! Nothing is my own, so what of it! Everything belongs to God. May He dispose all as best pleases Him.

Chapter IX, page 87, says: «Will Our Lady appear again? I don't expect she will», etc. I was referring to the Apparitions on the 13th, in the form they had taken in the preceding months. It was in this sense that I understood the question. [23]

There is another question also that has often been put to me, and to which I gave no answer other than silence or a smile. Dr. Antero de Figueiredo asked this question several times, and I answered in as few words as possible.

He was completely at a loss to understand my manner of acting, and that was what I wanted.

Almost all who questioned me were most impressed by the fact that, even while I was being interrogated, I lowered my eyes and concentrated my thoughts in such a way that I seemed to pay no attention to the question that was being put to me. At times, people even repeated their question, thinking that I had not heard it. I told Dr. Antero de Figueiredo that I was recalling what had happened with regard to the subject on which he had questioned me. And indeed that was true. But the real motive behind my action was that I was seeking, in the depths of my conscience and with the help of the Holy Spirit, an answer which, without revealing the reality, would still be in accordance with the truth.

V. JACINTA'S REPUTATION FOR SANCTITY

One Last Question

There remains one more question of Dr. Galamba's, which I have yet to answer: «How did people feel when they were in Jacinta's presence?» It is not easy to reply, for, ordinarily, I do not know what goes on within other people, and therefore I do not know how they feel. This means that I can only say what I felt myself, and describe any exterior manifestation of other people's feelings.

Jacinta, Reflection of God

What I myself usually felt was much the same as anyone feels in the presence of a holy person who seems to be in continual communication with God. Jacinta's demeanour was always serious and reserved, but friendly. All her actions seemed to reflect the presence of God in the way proper to people of mature age and great virtue. I never noticed in her that excessive frivolity or childish enthusiasm for games and pretty things, so typical of small children. This, of course, was after the Apparitions; before then, she was the personification of enthusiasm and caprice! I cannot say that the other children gathered around her as they did around me.

This was probably due to the fact that she did not know as many songs or stories with which to teach and amuse them, or perhaps that there was in her a seriousness far beyond her years.

If in her presence a child, or even a grown-up, were to say or do anything unseemly, she would reprimand them, saying:

«Don't do that, for you are offending the Lord our God, and He is already so much offended!»

If, as sometimes happened, the child or adult answered back, and called her a «pious Mary» or a plaster saint, or some other such thing, she would look at them very seriously and walk away without a single word. Perhaps this was one of the reasons why she did not enjoy more popularity. If I was with her, dozens of children would gather round us in no time; but if I went away, she would soon find herself all alone. Yet when I was with her, they seemed to delight in her company. They would hug and kiss her in the affectionate way of innocent children. They loved to sing and play with her, and sometimes begged me to go and look for her when she had not come out to play. If she told them that she did not want to come because they were naughty, they promised to be good if only she would come out:

«Go and get her, and tell her that we promise to be good if she'll come.»

When I went to visit her during her illness, I often found a large group waiting at the door, hoping to be able to come in with me and see her. They seemed to be held back by a certain sense of respect. Sometimes, before I left, I asked her:

«Jacinta, do you want me to tell some of them to stay here with you and keep you company?»

«Oh, yes! But just the ones who are smaller than myself.»

Then they all vied with each other, saying: «I'll stay! I'll stay!» After that, she entertained them by teaching them the Our Father, the Hail Mary, how to bless themselves, and to sing. Sitting on her bed or, if she was up, on the floor of the living-room, they played «pebbles», using crab apples, chestnuts, sweet acorns, dried figs and so on, all of which my aunt was only too happy to supply, so that her little girl might enjoy the children's company.

She prayed the Rosary with them, and counselled them not to commit sin, and so avoid offending the Lord our God and going to hell. Some of them spent whole mornings and afternoons with her, and seemed very happy in her company. But once they had left her presence, they did not dare to go back in the trusting way so natural to children. Sometimes they came in search of me, begging me to go in with them, or they waited for me outside the house, or else they waited at the door until my aunt or Jacinta herself invited them in to see her. They seemed to like her and to enjoy her company, but they felt themselves held back by a certain shyness or respect that kept them somewhat at a distance.

Jacinta, Model of Virtue

Grown-ups also went to visit her. They showed clearly how much they admired her demeanour, which was always the same, always patient, without being in the least demanding or complaining. Whatever the position in which she was lying when her mother left her, this was how she remained. If they asked her whether she felt better, she answered: «I'm just the same», or «I think I'm worse, thank you very much». There was an air of sadness about her, as she lay silent in the presence of visitors. People stayed sitting by her bedside for long periods at a stretch, and looked as though they felt happy to be there. It was there also that Jacinta had to undergo detailed and exhausting interrogations. She never showed the slightest impatience or repugnance, but merely told me later:

«My head aches so much after listening to all those people! Now that I cannot run away and hide, I offer more of these sacrifices to Our Lord.»

The neighbours sometimes brought along clothes they were making, so that they could sit and sew by her bedside.

«I'll work a little beside Jacinta,» they would say; «I don't know what it is about her, but it is good to be with her.»

They brought their little ones along too. The children amused themselves by playing with Jacinta, and their mothers were thus left free to do their sewing.

When people asked her questions, she answered in a friendly manner, but briefly. If they said anything which she thought improper, she promptly replied:

«Don't say that; it offends the Lord our God.»

If they related something unbecoming about their families, she answered:

«Don't let your children commit sin, or they could go to hell.»

If there were grown-ups involved, she said:

«Tell them not to do that, for it is a sin. They offend the Lord our God, and later they could be damned.»

People who came to visit us from a distance, either out of curiosity or from devotion, seemed to sense something supernatural about Jacinta. At times, when they came to my house to speak to me, they remarked:

«We've just been talking to Jacinta and Francisco; when with them we feel that there is something supernatural about them.»

Sometimes, they went so far as to want me to explain why they felt like that. As I did not know, I simply shrugged my shoulders and said nothing. I have often heard people commenting on this.

One day, two priests and a gentleman came to my home. While my mother was opening the door and inviting them to come in and sit down, I climbed into the attic to hide. My mother, after showing them in, left them alone, while she went out into the yard to call me, for she had left me there but a moment before. Not finding me, she delayed a while searching for me. In the meantime, the good gentlemen were discussing the matter:

«We'll see what this one will tell us.»

«What impressed me,» remarked the gentleman, «was the innocence and sincerity of Jacinta and her brother. If this one does not contradict herself, I'll believe. I don't know what it is I felt in the presence of those two children!»

«It's as though one feels something supernatural in their presence,» added one of the priests.

«It did my soul good to talk to them.»

My mother did not find me, and the good gentleman had to resign themselves to taking their departure without having been able to speak to me.

«Sometimes,» my mother told them, «she goes off to play with other children, and nobody can find her.»

«We're very sorry! We greatly enjoyed talking to the two little ones, and we wanted to talk to your little girl as well; but we shall come back another time.»

One Sunday, my friends from Moita, Maria, Rosa and

Ana Caetano, and Maria and Ana Brogueira, came after Mass to ask my mother to let me go and spend the day with them. Once I received permission, they asked me to bring Jacinta and Francisco along too. I asked my aunt and she agreed, and so all three of us went to Moita. After dinner, Jacinta was so sleepy that her little head began to nod. Mr. José Alves sent one of his nieces to go and put her to bed. In just a short while, she fell fast asleep. The people of the little hamlet began to gather in order to spend the afternoon with us. They were so anxious to see Jacinta that they peeped in to see if she were awake. They were filled with wonder when they saw that, although in a deep sleep, she had a smile on her lips, the look of an angel, and her little hands joined and raised towards heaven. The room was soon filled with curious people. Everyone wanted to see her, but those inside were in no hurry to come out and make room for the others. Mr. José Alves, his wife and his nieces all said:

«This must be an angel.»

Overcome, as it were, with awe, they remained kneeling beside the bed until, about half-past four, I went to call her, so that we could go and pray the Rosary in the Cova da Iria and then return home. Mr. José Alves' nieces are the Caetano girls mentioned above.

Francisco was Different

In contrast to Jacinta, Francisco was quite different. He had an easy manner, and was always friendly and smiling, playing with all the children without distinction. He did not rebuke anybody. All he did was to go aside, whenever he saw anything that was not as it should be. If he was asked why he went away, he answered:

«Because you're not good», or

«Because I don't want to play any more.»

During his illness, the children ran in and out of his room with the greatest freedom, talked to him through the window and asked him if he was feeling better, and so forth. If he was asked whether he wanted some of the children to stay with him and keep him company, he used to say that he preferred not, as he liked to be alone. He would say to me sometimes:

«I just like having you here, and Jacinta too.»

When grown-ups came to see him, he remained silent, only answering when directly questioned, and then in as few words as possible. People who came to visit him, whether they were neighbours or strangers, often spent long periods sitting by his bedside, and remarked:

«I don't know what it is about Francisco, but it feels so good to be here!»

Some women from the village commented on this one day to my aunt and my mother, after having spent quite a long time in Francisco's room:

«It's a mystery one cannot fathom! They are children just like any others, they don't say anything to us, and yet in their presence one feels something one can't explain, and that makes them different from all the rest »

«It seems to me that when we go into Francisco's room, we feel just as we do when we go into a church,» said one of my aunt's neighbours, a woman named Romana, who apparently did not believe in the Apparitions. There were three others in this group also: the wives of Manuel Faustino, José Marto and José Silva.

I am not surprised that people felt like that, being accustomed to find in everyone else only the preoccupation with material things which goes with an empty, superficial life. Indeed, the very sight of these children was enough to lift their minds to our heavenly Mother, with whom the children were believed to be in communication; to eternity, for they saw how eager, joyful and happy they were at the thought of going there; to God, for they said that they loved Him more than their own parents; and even to hell, for the children warned them that people would go there if they continued to commit sin. Externally, they were, so to speak, children like all others. But if these good people, so accustomed to the material side of life, had only known how to elevate their minds a little, they would have seen without difficulty that, in these children, there was something that marked them out as being different from all others.

I have just remembered something else connected with Francisco, and I am going to relate it here.

A woman called Mariana, from Casa Velha, came one day into Francisco's room. She was most upset because her husband had driven their son out of the house, and she was asking for the grace that her son would be reconciled with his father. Francisco said to her in reply:

«Don't worry. I'm going to heaven very soon, and when I get there I will ask Our Lady for that grace.»

I do not recall just how many days remained before he took his flight to heaven, but what I do remember is that, on the very afternoon of Francisco's death, the son went for the very last time to ask pardon of his father, who had previously refused it because his son would not submit to the conditions imposed. The boy accepted everything that the father demanded, and peace reigned once again in that home. This boy's sister, Leocadia by name, later married a brother of Jacinta and Francisco, and became the mother of their niece, whom Your Excellency met in the Cova da Iria when she was about to enter the Dorotheans.

EPILOGUE

I think, Your Excellency, that I have written everything that you have asked of me for now. Up to this, I did all I could to conceal the more intimate aspects of Our Lady's Apparitions in the Cova da Iria. Whenever I found myself obliged to speak about them, I was careful to touch on the subject very lightly, to avoid revealing what I wanted so much to keep hidden. But now that obedience has required this of me, here it is! I am left like a skeleton, stripped of everything, even of life itself, placed in the National Museum to remind visitors of the misery and nothingness of all passing things. Thus despoiled, I shall remain in the museum of the world, reminding all who pass, not of misery and nothingness, but of the greatness of the Divine Mercies.

May the Good God and the Immaculate Heart of Mary deign to accept the humble sacrifices which they have seen fit to ask of me, in order to vivify in souls the spirit of faith, confidence and love.

Tuy, 8th December, 1941

1. She is writing in the attic of the Novitiate House at Tuy.
2. This prologue reveals Lucia's literary taste and education, and shows that she had a rare talent for writing.
3. Lucia, however, never intended to say that she felt «inspired» in the scriptural sense of the word.
4. He was Lucia's cousin on her father's side.
5. It may well be said that Francisco had the gift of highest contemplation.
6. On August 11th, Lucia was taken by her father to appear before the Administrator.
   Ti Marto, however, refused to take his children there.
7. He refers to the Apparitions in June and July. They saw Our Lord in the mysterious light which Our Lady communicated to them.
8. Dangerous cliffs on the Atlantic coast off Portugal.
9. The observation was made by Lucia herself.
10. The following day was the 4th of April, 1919, at 10 a.m.
11. This is the reason why Lucia does not write down the third part of the secret here.
12. This «seventh time» refers to the 16th of June, 1921, on the eve of Lucia's departure to Vilar de Oporto. The Apparition in question had a personal message for Lucia, which she did not consider necessary to relate here.
13. This could mean «a long time».
14. Because she was in a hurry, Lucia omitted the end of the paragraph which, in other documents, reads as follows. «I promise salvation to those who embrace it, and those souls will be loved by God like flowers placed by me to adorn His throne.»
15. This was the aurora borealis on the night of January 25th to 26th, 1938, which was unusual, and always regarded by Lucia as the God-given sign which had been promised.
16. See Appendix 1.
17. See Appendix 2.
18. Lucia is mistaken in thinking that the Apparition happened on the same day on which they returned from the prison at Vila Nova de Ourém. This was not correct. The Apparition took place on the following Sunday, 19th August.
19. Lucia did not really mean to say that the war would be over on the same day; she was led to do so by the many pressing questions she was asked.
20. This is the second Brazilian edition.
21. This is the big holmoak which was left as it was, at the time of the Apparitions.
22. This interrogation took place in the house at Pontevedra from 16th to 20th September, 1935, inclusive. Antero de Figueiredo (1886-1935) uses that interrogation for his famous book: «Fatima: Graces, Secrets, Mysteries» (Lisbon 1936).
23. We have already mentioned that, as far as Lucia is concerned, the «seventh time» or other subsequent appearances are irrelevant here.

APPENDIX I

Fourth Memoir, note 16: Lucia writes, in the third person, this account of Our Lady's request for the Communion of Reparation on the First Saturdays.

On December 17th, 1927, she went before the tabernacle to ask Jesus how she should comply with what had been asked of her, that is, to say if the origin of the devotion to the Immaculate Heart of Mary was included in the Secret that the most holy Virgin had confided to her.

Jesus made her hear very distinctly these words: «My daughter, write what they ask of you. Write also all that the most holy Virgin revealed to you in the Apparition, in which she spoke of this devotion. As for the remainder of the Secret, continue to keep silence.»

What was confided on this subject in 1917, is as follows:

She asked for them to be taken to heaven, and the most holy Virgin answered: «Yes. I will take Jacinta and Francisco soon. But you are to stay here some time longer. Jesus wishes to make use of you to make me known and loved. He wants to establish in the world devotion to my Immaculate Heart. I promise salvation to those who embrace it, and these souls will be loved by God, like flowers placed by me to adorn His throne.»

«Am I to stay here all alone?» she asked, sadly.

«No, daughter. I shall never forsake you. My Immaculate Heart will be your refuge and the way that will lead you to God.»

On December 10th, 1925, the most holy Virgin appeared to her, and by her side, elevated on a luminous cloud, was a child. The most holy Virgin rested her hand on her shoulder, and as she did so, she showed her a heart encircled by thorns, which she was holding in her other hand. At the same time, the Child said:

«Have compassion on the Heart of your most holy Mother, covered with thorns, with which ungrateful men pierce it at every moment, and there is no one to make an act of reparation to remove them.»

Then the most holy Virgin said:

«Look, my daughter, at my Heart, surrounded with thorns with which ungrateful men pierce me at every moment by their blasphemies and ingratitude. You at least try to

191

console me and say that I promise to assist at the hour of death, with the graces necessary for salvation, all those who, on the first Saturday of five consecutive months, shall confess, receive Holy Communion, recite five decades of the Rosary, and keep me company for fifteen minutes while meditating on the fifteen mysteries of the Rosary, with the intention of making reparation to me.»

On February 15th, 1926, the Infant Jesus appeared to her again. He asked her if she had already spread the devotion to His most holy Mother. She told Him of the confessor's difficulties, and said that Mother Superior was prepared to propagate it, but that the confessor had said that she, alone, could do nothing.

Jesus replied:

«It is true that your Superior alone can do nothing, but with my grace, she can do all.»

She placed before Jesus the difficulty that some people had about confessing on Saturday, and asked that it might be valid to go to confession within eight days. Jesus answered:

«Yes, and it could be longer still, provided that, when they receive Me, they are in the state of grace and have the intention of making reparation to the Immaculate Heart of Mary.»

She then asked:

«My Jesus, what about those who forget to make this intention?»

Jesus replied:

«They can do so at their next confession, taking advantage of the first opportunity to go to confession.»

JMJ

No dia 17-12-1927, foi junto do Sacrario
perguntar a Jesus como satisfaria o pedido
que lhe era feito se a origem da devoção ao
Imaculado Coração de Maria estava encerrada
no segredo que a S.S. Virgem lhe tinha confiado!
Jesus com voz clara fez-lhe ouvir estas pala-
vras, Minha filha escreve o que te pedem
e tudo que te revelou a S.S. Virgem na
aparição em que falou desta devoção escreve-o
também, quanto ao resto do segredo continua o
silêncio. O que em 1917 foi confiado a ste
respeito é o seguinte. Esta pediu para os levar
para o céu. A S.S. Virgem respondeu, sim,
a Jacinta e o Francisco levo-os em breve mas
tu Lucia ficas cá mais algum tempo, Jesus quer
servir-se de ti para me fazer conhecer e amar

193

Ele quer estabelecer no mundo a devoção ao meu
Imaculado Coração, a quem a abraçar prometo
a salvação e serão queridas de Deus (como) estas almas
como flores postas por mim a adornar o seu
trono. Fico cá sozinha? disse com tristeza. Não filha
Eu nunca te deixarei, o meu Imaculado Cora-
ção será o teu refúgio e o caminho que te
conduzirá até Deus.
Dia 10-12-1925, apareceu-lhe a S. S.
Virgem e ao lado suspenço em uma nuvem
luminosa um menino.
A S. S. Virgem pondo-lhe no hombro
a mão e mostrando ao mesmo tempo
um Coração que tinha na outra mão
cercado de espinhos.
Ao mesmo tempo disse o Menino

tem pena do Coração de tua S. S. Mãe que
esta coberto de espinhos que os homens ingra-
tos a todos os momentos lhe cravam
sem haver quem faça um acto de
reparação para os tirar.

Em seguida disse a S. S. Vir-
gem.

Olha minha filha o meu Cora-
ção cercado de espinhos que os homens
ingratos a todos os momentos me cravão
com blasfemeas e ingratidões, tu ame-
nos vê de me consolar e diz que.
todos aqueles que durante 5 mezes
ao 1º Sabado se confessarem re-
cebendo a Sagrada Communhão,
rezarem um terço e me fizeram

195

15 minutos de companhia meditando
nos 15 misterios do Rosario com o
fim de me desagravar. Eu pro-
meto assistir-lhes na hora da mor-
te com todas as graças necessarias para
a salvação dessas almas.

No dia 15-2-1926

Apareceu-lhe de novo o menino Jesus
Perguntou se já tinha espalhado a devoção
a sua S. S. Mãe?

Ela expos-lhe as dificuldades que tinha
o Confessor e que a Madre Superiora
estava pronta a propaga-la mas que
o confessor tinha dito que ela só nada
podia. Jesus respondeu: é verdade que a tua
Superiora só nada pode mas com a

minha graça pode tudo; apresentou a Jesus a dificuldade que tinham algumas almas em se confessar ao sabado e pediu para ser valida a confissão de 8 dias, Jesus respondeu sim pode ser de muitos mais ainda contanto que quando me receberem estejam em graças e que tenham a intenção de desagravar o Imaculado Coração de Maria.

Ela perguntou; mas Jesus as que se esquecerem de formar essa intenção.

Jesus respondeu; podem forma-la na outra confissão seguinte aproveitando a 1ª ocasião que tiverem de se confessar

APPENDIX II

Third Memoir, note 10: The text concerning the fulfilment of Our Lady's promise that she would come, is given here in Lucia's own words:

Rev. Fr. Gonçalves sometimes came to our chapel to hear confessions. I went to confession to him and, as I felt at ease with him, I continued to do so for the three years that he remained here as Assistant to the Fr. Provincial.

It was at this time that Our Lady informed me that the moment had come in which she wished me to make known to Holy Church her desire for the Consecration of Russia, and her promise to convert it. The communication was as follows:

13-6-1929. I had sought and obtained permission from my superiors and confessor to make a Holy Hour from eleven o'clock until midnight, every Thursday to Friday night. Being alone one night, I knelt near the altar rails in the middle of the chapel and, prostrate, I prayed the prayers of the Angel. Feeling tired, I then stood up and continued to say the prayers with my arms in the form of a cross. The only light was that of the sanctuary lamp. Suddenly the whole chapel was illumined by a supernatural light, and above the altar appeared a cross of light, reaching to the ceiling. In a brighter light on the upper part of the cross, could be seen the face of a man and his body as far as the waist; upon his breast was a dove of light; nailed to the cross was the body of another man. A little below the waist, I could see a chalice and a large host suspended in the air, on to which drops of blood were falling from the face of Jesus Crucified and from the wound in His side. These drops ran down on to the host and fell into the chalice. Beneath the right arm of the cross was Our Lady and in her hand was her Immaculate Heart. (It was Our Lady of Fatima, with her Immaculate Heart in her left hand, without sword or roses, but with a crown of thorns and flames). Under the left arm of the cross, large letters, as if of crystal clear water which ran down upon the altar, formed these words: «Grace and Mercy».

I understood that it was the Mystery of the Most Holy Trinity which was shown to me, and I received lights about this mystery which I am not permitted to reveal.

Our Lady then said to me:

«The moment has come in which God asks the Holy

Father, in union with all the Bishops of the world, to make the consecration of Russia to my Immaculate Heart, promising to save it by this means. There are so many souls whom the Justice of God condemns for sins committed against me, that I have come to ask reparation: sacrifice yourself for this intention and pray.»

I gave an account of this to the confessor, who ordered me to write down what Our Lady wanted done.

Later, in an intimate communication, Our Lord complained to me, saying:

«They did not wish to heed my request. Like the King of France, they will repent and do it, but it will be late. Russia will have already spread her errors throughout the world, provoking wars, and persecutions of the Church; the Holy Father will have much to suffer.»

CONTENTS

11. AFTER THE APPARITIONS

111. ILLNESS AND DEATH OF JACINTA

SECOND MEMOIR

1. BEFORE THE APPARITIONS

11. THE APPARITIONS

111. AFTER THE APPARITIONS

THIRD MEMOIR

THE ORIGINAL MANUSCRIPTS

In order to acquaint the reader with the Memoirs as written down in Portuguese by Sister Lucia, at the request of her Bishop, some fourteen pages in Lucia's own handwriting have been selected and photocopies inserted at relevant intervals throughout the book.

LEAGUE OF PRAYER AND SACRIFICE FOR THE BEATIFICATION OF FRANCISCO AND JACINTA

The Causes of Beatification of the servants of God, Francisco and Jacinta Marto, were introduced in 1949. The promotion of the diocesan process was entrusted to the Postulator who, in order to achieve the desired aim, founded in 1963 the League of Prayer and Sacrifice, which has been approved in more than five hundred dioceses throughout the world. The members of the League undertake the following obligations:

1. To practise the virtues which distinguished the servants of God, Francisco and Jacinta Marto.

2. To pray and make sacrifices, while asking God, through the intercession of the Immaculate Heart of Mary, for the Beatification of the Seers.

3. In spiritual and temporal difficulties, to have recourse to the servants of God, praying to either Francisco only or to Jacinta only — as their Causes are taken separately — for the graces needed, and for the miracles necessary for their Beatification.

Those who wish to be inscribed in the League should send their complete name and address, in block letters, to the following address:

Postulation Centre,
Apartado 6,
Fatima, Portugal.

The League publishes a bulletin every two months which gives information regarding the Causes of Beatification of the Seers, and uses every possible means to promote devotion to the servants of God, Francisco and Jacinta Marto. This bulletin is issued in seven languages — English, Portuguese, Spanish, French, Italian, German and Hungarian. In order to cover expenses and ensure its continued publication, offerings small and large are gratefully accepted. The bulletin is sent to all who request it.

Fr. Louis Kondor, SVD

Postulator.

Printed in GRÁFICA ALMONDINA — Torres Novas (PORTUGAL)